# TRUTH IMAGINED

*Books by Eric Hoffer*

The True Believer

The Passionate State of Mind

The Ordeal of Change

The Temper of Our Time

Working and Thinking on the Waterfront

First Things, Last Things

Reflections on the Human Condition

In Our Time

Before the Sabbath

Between the Devil and the Dragon

Truth Imagined

# ERIC HOFFER

# TRUTH
# IMAGINED

HARPER & ROW, PUBLISHERS, New York
Cambridge, Philadelphia, San Francisco, London
Mexico City, São Paulo, Sydney

1817

*Designer: Sidney Feinberg*

Library of Congress Cataloging in Publication Data

Hoffer, Eric.
  Truth imagined.

    1. Hoffer, Eric.    2. Social reformers—United States—Biography.
3. Longshoremen—United States—Biography.
I.  Title.
HN64.H645    1983    303.4′85  [B]      83–47914
ISBN  0–06–015215–X

  84 85 86 87 10 9 8 7 6 5 4 3 2

*To Gemma*

TRUTH IMAGINED

IT IS CURIOUS how blurred my childhood memories are. I lost my sight at the age of seven. Two years before, my mother and I fell down a flight of stairs. She did not recover and died in that second year after the fall. I lost my sight and for a time my memory. I heard my father speak of me as an "idiot child."

All I remember about my mother is that she was small and always afraid. She must have loved her big five-year-old son to have carried him in her arms. Sometimes I wake up in the darkness and feel the pressure of her fingers on my back.

I have one vivid memory from early childhood and one from the age of nine. I remember that when I became restless my mother and Martha placed me on a table against a bookcase built into the wall. My father was a self-educated cabinetmaker and had nearly a hundred books, in English and German, on philosophy, mathematics, botany, chemistry, music, and travel. I spent passionate hours sorting the books according to size, thickness, and the color of their covers. I also learned to distinguish between English and German books. Eventually I could sort according to contents. I might say, therefore, that I had learned to read both English and German before I was five. The passion to sort had one other vital consequence. When I began to think and write I discovered that I was still sorting—sorting facts and impressions and collating them.

The other vivid memory is of hearing Beethoven's Ninth

Symphony at the age of nine. My father drove me in a cab to a concert hall in New York. Usually subdued, my father was strangely excited. He loved music and was thoroughly familiar with the Beethoven work we were about to hear. The Ninth Symphony, he said, which Beethoven composed while deaf, was a tapestry of heavenly melodies. He hummed some of them. The third movement in particular, he said, was sublime. I cannot remember how long the concert lasted. When the third movement of the Ninth was played, my father gripped my arm and I soared as if I had wings.

Later, when I regained my sight and went out into the world, I found myself humming the third movement whenever I felt alone and abandoned. When I finally settled in San Francisco in 1941, the first thing I did was to buy a phonograph and records of the Ninth. I found that no record played the third movement the way I remembered. They played it too fast and offhandedly to convey its pleading sadness.

I regained my sight at the age of fifteen. I never took the trouble to learn the causes of the sudden loss and return of sight. Martha said jokingly that it was a miracle the Hoffers managed to stay alive. None of them lived past fifty. "Never worry about the future, Eric—you'll be dead by the time you are forty." Her words sank into my mind and became a source of lightheartedness during my years as a migratory worker. I went through life like a tourist.

It is also remarkable that I lacked the curiosity to find out what Martha's relation was to my family. Was she a relative or a paid housekeeper? I was immersed in her loving care. She encouraged me to talk and seemed to remember everything I said. My memories of her are mainly of touch and smell. The aroma of her large body is still in my nostrils, and I still remember the touch of her firm breasts with nipples like fingers. She insisted on speaking broken English to save me from isolation in an English-speaking country. I acquired her accent. During severe headaches she would take me in her arms, pass her lips over my face, and hum wordless lullabies. The regaining of sight brought this enormous intimacy to an end. My sense of loss was mitigated by a plunge into an orgy of reading.

As I said, I learned to read before I was five. When my sight returned I could read fluently. I did not worry about straining my eyes, since I was sure that the regaining of sight was temporary. I wanted to read all I could before going blind again. There was a secondhand bookstore down the street. The first thing I saw one day when I entered the small store was the word "Idiot" in golden letters. The word jumped at me from an upper shelf. My father's reference to me as an "idiot child" alerted me to the word. What I had was Dostoevski's *The Idiot*. I have been rereading the book every year since. The storytelling of the first chapters is unsurpassed. The store also had many translations from Scandinavian languages and from German.

My father died in 1920, not quite fifty. Martha left for Germany right after the war. She was not happy after I regained my sight. I do not remember whether she wrote to us. My father was a member of a brotherhood of cabinetmakers. The brotherhood buried him and gave me three hundred dollars. I decided to go to California, where it was warm enough for a man to sleep outside and oranges grew along the roads. I arrived in Los Angeles in April 1920.

I WAS ALONE in the world, yet not afraid. I was totally igno-
rant of the mechanics of earning a living and did not worry
about what would happen when the three hundred dollars
were gone. I rented a cheap room near the Los Angeles Pub-
lic Library and spent every minute reading. It did not occur
to me to explore the city. I lived frugally. When the money
was spent I sold my clothes, including a leather jacket, for a
pittance and finally faced the mysterious thing called hunger.
What happens when one does not eat? I knew that people die
of hunger. How long can they go without food? Is death
waiting? On the third day of hunger it was as if a hand
squeezed and wrung my stomach and pushed it upward
against my chest. When I drank water, my scalp tingled as if
stung by a swarm of bees. I still had my room and each
evening I bathed. There was a feeling of pity for my own
body, and I kept it scrupulously clean. I noticed that the hair
seemed to grow faster than usual.

I kept walking, for I could not endure sitting down for
more than a few minutes. I was afraid of my own thoughts. I
kept wondering why, although the body had been without
fuel, my legs kept moving and my hair grew so fast. I paid no
attention to the display of food in restaurant windows. I had
no reveries of food, but every night in my dreams I smelled
the fragrance of the fried chopped meat Martha used to cook.

Once I caught a glimpse of my face in a store mirror. It
was a face distorted with anxiety. I felt surprised. I was whol-

ly absorbed in the wonder of hunger and banned all thought
about myself.

On the evening of the third day I stopped in front of a pet
shop on Main Street. In an enclosure behind the glass of the
show window were pigeons. Some were white, some gray,
and two were white with a chocolate band around their
necks. There seemed to be a grouping according to color. The
two with the chocolate bands were near the glass. One was
tiny and the other big. The tiny one lifted its beak and
pushed it into the beak of the big one, and with clasped beaks
they swayed their heads from side to side. I thought I was
watching an act of feeding—the big one feeding the little
one. But I immediately changed my mind. For there was an
ecstasy and obliviousness of everything in the swaying of the
heads, with half-closed eyes and the impatient stamping of
the pink feet. They separated and the big one strutted in a
circle around the tiny one. I knew then that I was witnessing
the ritual which precedes the act of mating. The tiny one
inflated her body, pulled in her head, closed her eyes and
flattened herself against the wooden floor. Then with a flutter
of wings the big one perched on her and pushed his beak into
her neck feathers, and the two bodies rocked and swayed.
The air was charged with an eagerness which knows no ending.

I suddenly realized that in watching the pigeons I forgot
my hunger. The realization filled me with wonder. It seemed
strange that hunger was a mere sensation, like toothache, and
that by diverting one's attention one could forget it. I suddenly felt light and free. It was as if I had awakened from a
nightmare. That night I ate. I entered a restaurant and volun-
teered to scrub pots for a meal. Hunger lost its awe.

The elderly dishwasher showed me how to deal with the
pots and we got to talking. The way to get a job, he said, was

to go down to the State Free Employment Agency on skid row, at the foot of Fifth Street. There were many jobless people, but I would have the same chance as the others.

I followed his advice, and thus almost overnight I was transferred from the nursery to the gutter.

3

THE dispatching hall of the State Free Employment Agency was a former garage. The unemployed occupied rows of benches facing a screened platform. One would hear a telephone ring behind the screen and soon a clerk would step out and over a loudspeaker call for a man to move furniture, wash dishes, wash windows, and so on. Up went a forest of hands and the clerk picked one hand. Enough jobs kept coming in to keep the men hopeful. I had a seat on one of the front benches and in the afternoon finally got a job to mow a lawn.

By sticking to my seat from early morning to late afternoon, I earned enough to keep me going. I had time to read and to muse. There was something that needed explaining. It took the clerk a few seconds to call out the job and a few seconds to pick a hand. Surely there was not time enough for the clerk to weigh anything in his mind before he picked a specific hand. There must be something in the outside world that made up his mind ·for him. If I knew what that something was, I could manipulate the clerk. I tried all sorts of things. I found that the clerk's eyes often skipped the front five rows and landed on the middle of the sixth. A book wrapped in red paper arrested the clerk's attention. I tried different facial expressions. I found that when raising my hand I must look as if I had not a worry in the world. Cheerfulness attracts attention. With these arrangements I was sure to bag several jobs a day. I felt secure.

Things went on like this for years. I lived frugally, read endlessly, and began to educate myself by reading college textbooks on mathematics, chemistry, physics, and geography. I acquired the habit of keeping notebooks to aid my memory. I was developing a passion for painting with words and spent endless hours searching for the right adjective.

I also got to talking with the people around me. America before the coming of F.D.R. was singularly free of self-pity. None of the people I talked with blamed anyone for their misfortune. Almost without exception they prefaced their life stories with a ritualistic "I have no one to blame but myself." There were many immigrants, and talking to them I learned a lot about the countries they came from.

It was reasonable to assume that I would continue to live the way I did until I died at forty. It was a satisfactory, full life. However, permanence was not a characteristic of the America I was living in. In the late 1920s jobs became scarce. There was a financial crisis and factories laid off workers. I had to try something new. Still coming in every morning were calls for men to sell oranges. I had heard these calls for years and was never tempted. I did not believe I could sell anything. Now I paid attention: "Men to peddle oranges, twenty-five cents on the dollar, paid every evening, free lunch, boss outside." I went out to have a look at the trucks. My attention was immediately arrested by a lightweight truck with side curtains rolled up and with a glittering heap of oranges in the back. The owner, a slim, darkish man with a southern accent, urged us to come and get it. It was easy money, no sweating. He needed four peddlers. I climbed into the truck with three other fellows and the owner (Blackie) drove us to Westwood, a suburb of Los Angeles made up of rows upon rows of identical small homes. He gave each of us two buckets filled with oranges and told us to go knock on the back doors. We each had a row of houses.

The first back door was opened by a middle-aged woman. She said, "Yes?" I was frozen stiff and could not open my mouth. I merely stretched out my hands with the buckets. A smile appeared on the woman's face. She said, "Come in, come in, I'll take both buckets." To cover my confusion I cleaned out the vegetable bin, lined it with clean paper, and laid out the oranges, the hard ones at the bottom and the ripe ones on top to be eaten first. Blackie refilled my buckets and I knocked on the next door. The woman who opened the door was all smiles; she was waiting for me. The neighbor must have called her up to alert her to the tongue-tied peddler who cleaned the bins and stacked the oranges like a work of art. It went on like this in house after house. Blackie was behind me all the time, cheering me on with "Get hot, Eric." He began to believe that I would singly sell the load. I found my tongue and began to pay outrageous compliments to the housewives. Nobody could resist me. Then one woman asked me whether I raised my own oranges. I described an imagined farm and my family. We ran out of oranges in the early afternoon.

As I sat down to eat my lunch and count the money, I became aware of a deep misgiving. It was something I never felt before—shame. I was frightened by my readiness to lie, to say and probably do anything to make a sale. It was evident that in my case selling was a source of corruption. I might kill people in the street to make a sale. Perhaps I was corruptible in general and had to learn how to avoid temptation.

Blackie blew his top when I told him that I was not coming back.

I RETURNED to the hall. The jobs were scarce, but by being in the hall most of the day I picked up enough work to keep me going. I was a conscientious worker and some employers asked for my telephone number in order to call me when they had a job to do. Since I had no phone, I suggested that when they called the hall they ask for me by name. I prayed for a steady job.

One day I was dispatched to a pipe yard on Santa Fe Avenue. The yard was selling secondhand pipe to independent oil men. The owner of the yard was a small, lively man by the name of Shapiro. At that time I was not as curious about ethnic backgrounds as I am now. I distinguished between blacks, whites, Mexicans, and Chinese. I did not recognize Shapiro as a Jewish name. All during the day I was aware of Shapiro's searching eyes. I wondered whether he would order me back. Work in the pipe yard was not hard and sometimes interesting. In the evening Shapiro ordered all of us back. I was surprised to hear him address me by name. Did I like the work? Did I have enough money to eat? It was necessary that I eat well, drink milk. He gave me a twenty-dollar advance.

It was my first steady job. I loved the routine of work, reading, and studying. The camaraderie with Shapiro was not unusual. Bosses and workers in this country show such a camaraderie when they talk about sports or politics. Shapiro talked to me about books. He was interested in what I was reading. I learned that he had had an academic education and would have had an academic career, but an uncle left the yard to him when he died. So, instead of becoming a professor, Shapiro became a superior junkman. The closure of the yard on Yom Kippur made me aware of Shapiro's Jewishness. I started to read books about the Jews. I was convinced it was his Jewishness that made Shapiro notice me. The Jews, I learned, were a peculiar people. They discovered God, and their role in history had been out of proportion to their number. Unlike other gods, the Jewish God is not an idle aristocrat but a hardworking master mechanic. Only in the Occident, which worshiped such a God and tried to imitate him, could a machine age originate. The Chinese and the Japanese, despite their ingenuity and capacity for mastering skills, could not invent a machine age. They had to receive it from the West. Shapiro was delighted with the idea and urged me to write it down. I liked to listen to him speak about the Jews. He mentioned the fact that the Jews were from the beginning a literate people. There has never been a Jew who could not read. It occurred to me that only in such a society could plain workingmen like Jesus and the apostles launch a new religion.

The Jews, a very ancient people, were outstanding in their capacity for deciphering the hieroglyphs of the human face. Whatever a man does and thinks inscribes itself on his face. Man's face is an open book which reveals all his secrets, but the writing is hieroglyphic and only a few people have a key to decipher it. My preoccupation with the Jews grew with the years.

Shapiro suggested that I read Renan's *History of the People of Israel*. The book, in five volumes, was hard to get but Shapiro had it in his library. Hardly anyone reads Renan's history at present. Renan's reputation as a historian is not high. He is accused of psychologizing too much. And, indeed,

Renan's *History of the People of Israel* is a brilliant commentary on the human condition. His passionate preoccupation with man's soul made Renan a good prophet. His observations are timeless; they shed more light on the contemporary situation than do the writings of our foremost thinkers.

In 1930 I was twenty-eight years old. I had been with Shapiro for two years and it was reasonable to assume that if I died at forty, as Martha had predicted, I would be spending the rest of my life in Shapiro's yard. But Shapiro died in 1930 of pneumonia. To me the death of Shapiro seemed a fateful culmination. I had saved some money and I decided to stop working for a year until the money was spent—time enough to figure out what I would do with my remaining years.

IT WAS my first vacation. Monday I loitered in the streets of the town amidst people rushing in a frenzy of business, and I felt neither guilty nor restless. I was a ladybird among ants. I remembered reading somewhere that people who achieved much first discovered their life's goal at the age of twenty-seven. In other words, twenty-seven is a crucial year in great lives. It amused me to think that, although there was no sign of future achievement, I took time off at twenty-eight to discover what I might do in the years ahead.

I suddenly felt a desire to reread some of the books I had read when I regained my eyesight. I reread Hamsun, Lagerlöf, and Dostoevski. I knew Dostoevski's *The Idiot* almost by heart, but his other books I had read only once. Rereading *Crime and Punishment* and *The Brothers Karamazov*, I realized that in the intervening years my mind had matured. I now derived intense pleasure from details I had not noticed during the first reading. Somehow the first reading of Dostoevski left an impression of gloom. Now I felt an undercurrent of mirth permeating even the gloomiest episodes. In rereading *Crime and Punishment* I was now vaguely conscious of a wonderful art of construction, as of a high, vaulted edifice in which the numerous distinct details enhance the impression of a monumental whole. And how wonderful his art of creating living beings. The probings and descriptions, though brilliant, are few. It is by the words of their mouth that the characters burst into life. A few spoken words, and there before you are persons more alive than the majority of people around you, and you know them more intimately than you know close relatives and friends. They are strange, extravagant beings, it is true, unlike people in this country, and probably unlike persons anywhere, including Russia. But they are made up of the essence of humanness, and however eccentric and outlandish, they are close to our heart and understanding. There is a grandeur in Dostoevski's extremes. They give us a glimpse of an explosive at the core of the human entity, of the enormous distance between the unknown depths and the familiar surface of our daily existence.

One book, however, dominated my mind during those days. It was the Old Testament. I had known of the book all my life, I was familiar with the names of its chief personages and with several of its tales, but in all my years I had not read one sentence of the text. Probably, being by nature devoid of any religious sense, I lacked the curiosity which would have prompted me to read the book I knew as the fountain of all religion. Now a new kind of curiosity tempted me to read it. Just as the consciousness of his swelling muscles drives a young man to test his strength at weight lifting and wrestling, so the consciousness that my mind had matured inclined me to tackle tasks I had not tried before.

Thus, armed with patience, I was willing to work my way through a landscape which could not but be tedious and unsympathetic. I was therefore completely unprepared for the onrush of impressions which burst upon me even as I read the opening sentences. What grandeur, vividness, and freshness of perception! A primitive mentality, naive, clumsy, yet bold and all-embracing, throbbing with an eager curiosity, sparked an imagination which had the directness, precision, and penetration of a grand scientific conception. What a passion for symmetry and order! Without the equipment of knowledge or tools, a bold mind sets itself to subdue the chaos of the multitude of natural phenomena, to correlate, intertwine, and arrange them into a pattern. Just as the scientific mind gives equally painstaking attention to the movement of the stars and the efforts of a blind worm, so here a primitive mind sets out to find the whys and wherefores of the skies, the oceans, the sun, the moon, and the stars, love, death, the pains of childbirth, the crawling of the snake, the enmity between man and the snake, the necessity to work, the presence of weeds and thorns, the enmity between the nomad and the tiller of the soil, the rainbow, the multitude of languages. Concerning the last it is written; "And the whole land was one language and one speech. And it came to pass as they journeyed from the East that they found a plain in the land of Shinar and they dwelt there. And they said one to another: 'Go to, let us make brick and burn them thoroughly.' And they had brick for stone, and slime had they for mortar. And they said: 'Go to, let us build us a city and a tower whose top may reach unto heaven, and let us make us a name—lest we be scattered abroad upon the face of the whole earth.' And the Lord came down to see the city and the tower which the children of men builded. And the Lord said: 'Behold the people is one, and they have all one language, and this they begin to do and now nothing will be restrained from them which they have imagined to do. Let us go down and there confound their language that they may not understand one another's speech.' So the Lord scattered them abroad from thence upon the face of all the earth, and they left off to build the city. Therefore is the name of it called Babel, because the Lord did there confound the language of all the earth."

The never-flagging imagination, so marvelous a tool, knowing no obstacles, feeds on the copious juice of human experience. Life throbs in every line of the book. The eager creativeness of the imagination of the unequaled storytellers is a goad to their powers of observation. Nothing is too slight for their attention: motives, acts, speech, dress, manners, and innumerable particulars are rendered with great vividness. There is everywhere evident a love of everyday reality. The good is taken with the bad. There is no touching-up to lend a false appearance of perfection. The great men have faults, and these are recorded with as much vividness and detail as accomplishments and virtues. The imagined truth of these storytellers is more alive, more true, than truth.

A society that accepts the life of man in its entirety and steeps itself with the strong juice of life is not given to sentimentality. Side by side with the exhortation not to afflict the widow and the orphan, not to oppress the stranger, and not to harden one's heart against the poor and the needy, there is the sober admonition not to favor the poor in his quarrel.

So absorbed were they in the reality of this world that ancient Jews gave no thought to a hereafter; no blessing exceeded life on this earth. The greatest reward was to have one's life prolonged. Not one word about a future life. "As the cloud is consumed and vanishes away, so he that goes down to the grave shall come up no more" (Job 7:9). "Man lies down and rises not till the heavens be no more, they shall not awake, nor be raised out of their sleep" (Job 14:12).

The truth imagined of Old Testament history is a palpitating body. All persons, whether heroes or lesser men, are of flesh and blood, real, human, so that after more than two thousand years they seem nearer and more familiar than the personages of our own history, even Washington and Lincoln. Moses talks, and you see him standing on the top of Mount Pisgah within sight of the Promised Land. The breeze ruffles his silver beard and his voice flutters over the sea of upturned faces. "The Lord was angry with me for your sakes and swore that I should not go over the Jordan, and that I should not go into the good land, which God gives you for an inheritance. But I must die in this land, I must not go over the Jordan, but you shall go over and possess the good land" (Deut. 4:21–22). King David, the darling of the writers of the history, is a fascinating mixture of manliness and feminine waywardness. He is bold, tricky, generous, selfish, lecherous, tenderhearted, overbearing, submissive, forgiving and vindictive, quick to sin and to repent; he is a cunning diplomat, an organizer, a poet, and a musician. He is equally ready with his sword, his harp, and his tears. He is praised and glorified, yet you know him for what he was—nothing has been retouched. His opponent, King Saul, is a big clumsy plowman forced into kingship, weighed down by his melancholy and forebodings. He is no match for the intriguing Samuel. Our heart goes out to him in the unequal struggle.

So, too, in the presentation of Jacob and Esau. Though the writer favors Jacob, the father of the race, and deprecates Esau, these characters unfold and have lives of their own. In spite of themselves the writers of the history depict Esau as a lovable person. He is a red-haired roughneck, a cunning hunter, a man of the field; he is hearty and good-natured. He has a ravenous appetite. When hungry, he will sell his soul for a meal. See him return from a fruitless hunt, tired and hungry. He finds Jacob—their mother's darling—cooking a savory dish of lentils. He asks for some of the red pottage. He waves away all haggling, and gives his birthright to Jacob for a dish of lentils. Indeed, Isaac, the blind old father, loved his boisterous, manly son. He loved the smell of the clothes, described "as the smell of the fields which God hath blessed" (Genesis 27:27). He loved the venison which the hunter brought and his talk of the hunt and the goings-on in a world he no longer could see. I wondered why the writers of the history picked the unlovely Jacob as the father of the race. Is it because a cautious, cunning Jacob has a higher capacity for survival than a reckless Esau? I also wondered whether most great men were the darlings of strong-willed mothers.

Even Ahab—king of the northern state of Israel, of whom the authors say that "There was none like unto Ahab which did sell himself to works of wickedness in the sight of Jehovah" (I Kings 21:25)—is depicted impartially, with much detail, and the result is that the wicked Ahab emerges as an attractive personality. He is of peasant stock, and his love is for fields and vineyards. He is tenderhearted. During a severe drought he "goes out into the land, unto all fountains of water and unto all brooks peradventure he may find grass to keep the horses and mules alive" (I Kings 18:5). He likes to have gardens around his palace. Near his palace is a vineyard owned by Naboth, the Jezreelite, and Ahab wants to make it a garden. Here is how he, an absolute king, goes about it. He says to Naboth, "Give me your vineyard that I may have it for a garden of herbs, because it is near unto my house and I will give you for it a better vineyard or if it seems good to you the worth of it in money" (I Kings 21:2). Naboth, a proud squire, refuses, saying, "God forbid that I should give the inheritance of my father unto thee" (I Kings 21:3). Ahab shows no temper. He does not call his henchmen to enforce his will but returns to the palace, lies down on his bed, turns his face, and eats no bread. It requires Jezebel, the daughter of an Oriental tyrant, to set in motion the simple intrigue by which the coveted vineyard is finally acquired. Clearly, Ahab is weak, but he is not evil. He is one of the most civilized personages depicted in the history. In his reign, the relations with the sister kingdom, Judah, to the south, are for the first time friendly and close. And when Ahab defeats the insolent

Ben-Hadad, king of Syria, he does not vent his vengeance but calls him brother and sends him home.

There are few persons mentioned in this book who have not the breath of life. Who can number the living hosts teeming in these pages: kings, priests, judges, counselors, soldiers, plowmen, laborers, traders, dervishes, prophets, witches, soothsayers, madmen, lepers. Has ever a literature woven so vast a panorama of life? Even minor personages referred to briefly here and there come alive and you know them intimately.

The language of the book is clumsy and disjointed. The same adjectives are used to describe the fat cows in Pharaoh's dream and the beautiful Rachel. Yet, somehow, the sentences sprout and bloom. To read even the code of laws is like walking through the countryside in spring. "Thou shalt not see thy brother's ox or his sheep go astray and hide thyself from them. . . . Thou shalt not see thy brother's ass or his ox fall down by the way and hide thyself from them; thou shalt surely help him to lift them up again. If a bird's nest chance to be before thee in any tree or on the ground, whether they be young ones or upon the eggs, thou shalt not take the dame with the young. But thou shalt take the young to thee, that it may be well with thee, and prolong thy days. When thou buildest a new house then thou shalt make a battlement for the roof, that thou bring not blood upon thy house if any man fall from thence" (Deuteronomy 22: 1-8).

It also occurred to me that the fact that the Jews were the world's first and unsurpassed storytellers might explain their present role as outstanding pioneers, as theoreticians in the sciences and social affairs. The capacity to imagine the truth, to visualize the unknown, to tell a story, is indispensable for exploring the unknown.

IT WAS surprising that now that I had quit work and the whole of each day was at my disposal, my waking hours were crowded with incessant activity. The vast town in which I had lived several years seemed now as if I was seeing it for the first time. I had a few inexpensive appetites. I liked beef stew cooked so that the chunks of juicy meat, small potatoes, and slices of carrots and parsnips were embedded in a thick red-brown gravy. A cafeteria on Hill Street excelled in the preparation of this stew, and I ate supper there daily. Of evenings, as I walked through the town to the library and my supper, my senses were like playful puppies probing and sniffing everything within reach. It was as if I could hear the life-beat of the vast city, and every pore of my body was conscious of the tenseness in the air over the crowded sidewalks. Yet, as my eyes raced toward the thousands of faces, they found nothing to linger on. The faces seemed vacant. In none of them was there an expression of joy or sadness, a hint of a buried preoccupation or a gnawing worry; none betrayed uncertainty or expectation. Of all the faces which I scanned my memory retains but three.

One, of a middle-aged woman standing on the edge of the sidewalk. The face was pale, almost translucent. The eyes expressed a quiet despair. She looked up and down the street, and it was evident that she expected no one, that it mattered not which way she went.

Next, the delicate face of a boy leaning over a puppy

which he held in his arms as if it were fragile and precious. The bright eyes and the face expressed wonderment, tenderness, pride, and fear. It was as if that very minute the boy had breathed life into an inert lump and lo, there in his arms was a warm, living puppy with a black snout, a red tongue, teeth, living eyes, the feel of ribs against his fingers, and a tail—a very dog indeed. But was life secure in the tiny lump? Would it stay there?

Finally, a woman in black entered the cafeteria one night as I was eating supper. She sat down at a table and looked around timidly. She was obviously a stranger in this city and perhaps a foreigner, for she did not know the workings of the cafeteria, where one served oneself. Her soft black eyes followed the hustling busboy who was clearing the tables, mistaking him for a waiter. I walked over to her table. She looked at me, frightened, and as I started to explain the manner in which meals were served she rose as if to leave. I praised the beef stew extravagantly and the hint of a smile appeared in the corners of her small mouth. I herded her gently toward the stack of trays, supervised the ordering of the meal, and then carried her loaded tray to her table. She looked uncomfortable and embarrassed. I said, "Madam, I am harmless, you should not mind me," and walked back to my table. She smiled again and all was well. Any impulse I might have had to get acquainted died stillborn. I sensed the mistrust dammed up in her mind. I gathered my books and bid her good night.

The routine of walking, eating, reading, studying, and scribbling continued week after week. I could have gone on like that all my remaining years. The thought that once the money was gone I would have to return to work, day in day out till death, filled me with weariness. What could it matter whether I died at the end of this year or ten years later? I wondered what would happen if I refused to return to work. Would I become a beggar or a thief? Were there other alternatives? In retrospect I can see that the idea of suicide was already hatching in the back of my mind. There was plenty of time to make up my mind.

As the end of 1931 approached, the time came to decide what I would do when the money was gone. Actually, my mind was already made up: I would commit suicide. All I had to do was to settle the details. I had to find the means of a quick, painless death. A revolver would have been ideal, but it was not to be had without a police permit. Gas might leak into adjoining rooms and alarm the neighbors. Death by jumping from a bridge or being run over seemed crude. There remained poison. The article on poison in the *Encyclopaedia Britannica* gave me all the information. The corrosive poisons, such as carbolic acid, which are the salts of heavy metals, destroy the intestines, act slowly, and cause much pain. The abrasive poisons, such as oxalic acid, are more subtle. They penetrate into the bloodstream. But they also attack the intestines and cause vomiting. The systemic poisons, such as potassium cyanide, affect the nervous system and bring about unconsciousness. They act rapidly and cause little pain. The same is more or less true of strong opiates such as Veronal. A round of several drugstores showed that no potassium cyanide was to be had. Veronal and other opiates were sold only on doctor's orders. I settled therefore on oxalic acid. The encyclopedia mentioned it as a common cause of accidental poisoning, since its crystals resemble those of Epsom salt, which has a wide use as a bleach. I bought a large quantity of oxalic acid for twenty-five cents. Thus in one day my task was done.

Mᴦ ʟᴀsᴛ ᴅᴀʏ was a Sunday. From the moment of waking I was conscious of a dark worry hammering on my brain. It dominated the room. The books on the table, the pots and plates in the corner did not meet my eye with the joyful familiarity of the days before. They looked like visiting friends who came inopportunely on a family quarrel; they turned their backs. What had happened? It was not the fact that I was to die in the evening, for death had no image or voice which on closer approach I could see or hear and be gripped with fear. Even as late as the small hours of the preceding night my mind was peaceful. I was rereading for hours the tales of Jacob and his sons, chuckling over the vivid details and marveling at the unsurpassed storytelling. Now I was like one lost in a dark forest; I dared not leave my bed. Thus, between gray drowsing and gloomy waking, I passed the hours until the black night raised itself to my window and beckoned me to come out. In retrospect, it is clear that the reason for the sudden worry that morning was simply the disappearance of a "tomorrow." Death would have no terror were it to come a month from now, a week, or even a day. For death's one terror is that it has no "tomorrow."

I poured the oxalic acid crystals into a bottle half full of water. Part of it dissolved and the rest settled on the bottom. I wrapped the bottle in a newspaper and went out into the street. My intention was to walk out beyond the city, where any cries of anguish would find no response, and if, driven by pain, I would rush back for help it would be of no avail, for a run of two miles or so would accelerate the working of the poison and put an end to all efforts.

I followed Figueroa Street southward. The bright sidewalks eased my mind. The restaurants were crowded. Waitresses in uniform fluttered about the tables and behind the counters. The clank of silver and the call of orders escaped into the warm night. Streetcars buzzed back and forth; they seemed like huge lanterns suspended from a wire. At a stopping place a middle-aged man and a boy were waiting for a streetcar. They were in the full light of a street lamp. I saw the boy raising himself on tiptoe to adjust the tie of the older man and to smooth the lapels of the dark suit, and all the while the boy talked eagerly. When done, he clasped the hand of the older man again and stamped his feet with joyous impatience.

Away from the center of the city the sidewalks were deserted. The small restaurants, far apart, were gathering places for the neighborhood families. Here and there brilliantly lit vegetable markets were glittering islands in the vast darkness.

I adjusted the bottle against my arm and thought feverishly, "It would be good if this street had no end—I would walk on forever, and my feet would never tire; neither would I fret, nor complain." I thought of roads winding through green fields and orchards, running out to the blue ocean. There seemed nothing so pleasant as walking on roads, legs and hands swinging, and the knapsack rocking gently. I did not know then that the sudden vision of life as an endless road was the first intimation of a revulsion against suicide.

By now I was walking on a dirt road. Oil derricks like gibbets suddenly loomed ahead of me. A tall eucalyptus tree stood alone in the field to the left of the road. I made for it, stumbling over rough ground. My thoughts ran on feverishly while I freed the bottle from its wrappings. I removed the stopper and took a mouthful. It was as if a million needles pricked the inside of my mouth. In a blaze of anger I spat the oxalic acid out, continued spitting and coughing, and while wiping my lips I let the bottle fly and heard its thud in the dark.

I hastened back to the road, still spitting and coughing. I ran on the dirt road, I reached the cement paving. The sound of my steps on the paved road was like the clapping of hands. I was in a fever of excitement and talked to myself. I kept running until I joined the crowd. The lamps, the flashing traffic signals, the ringing bells, the streetcars, the automobiles, all the handiwork of man seemed part of my flesh and bone. I walked toward the cafeteria tingling with a ravenous appetite.

As I swallowed my food the vision of life as a road—a winding, endless road that knows not where it goes and what its load—came back to me. Here was an alternative I had not thought of to the deadening routine of a workingman's life in the city. I must get out on the road which winds from town to town. Each town would be strange and new; each town would proclaim itself the best and bid me take my chance. I would take them all and never repent.

I did not commit suicide, but on that Sunday a workingman died and a tramp was born.

I SPENT the next ten years, from 1931 to the outbreak of the Second World War, on the road. When, after the failed suicide, I left Los Angeles with a small bundle slung over my shoulder, my heart was light. When the road reached the open country I knew that I had come home. I was without fear. There was no need for a period of adjustment. I was not going to thumb a ride or ride freight trains. If offered a ride, I would accept but I would not beg for one.

As I walked on briskly I began to compose a poem. Searching for words goes well with a swinging walk. I remember the first stanza:

> It is a thrill to walk alone
> Where fields sweep far to meet the sky
> And mountains float in dreamy blue
> And whispering winds in haste rush by

In the afternoon I was given a ride. The German-sounding driver said he was going to Anaheim. Where was I going? I told him that I had no destination, I was just walking. He disapproved. "A man must have a goal. It is not good to live without hope." He quoted Goethe: "Hope lost, all lost, it were better one never was born." I did not argue but in my heart I knew that if the driver quoted Goethe correctly then Goethe was a small potato. When we reached Anaheim I found my way to the small library. Strangely, the library had only Goethe's *Faust*. As I leafed through the book I felt like one looking for a needle in a haystack. Then I saw a thick volume on Goethe by George Brandeis. I found the quotation. The driver had misquoted. Goethe did not say hope (*Hoffnung*) lost, and so on, but courage (*Mut*) lost. As I came out of the library I saw a sign saying "Dishwasher wanted" in the window of a restaurant. I got the job.

The restaurant was owned by two brothers who did the cooking and worked in two shifts. In Los Angeles I had heard much talk about the evils of capitalism. Capitalist greed was blamed for the depression. My feeling was that capitalists could not possibly be of one kind. Now I had the chance to see two capitalists in action. What I found was that, although these two capitalists were brothers, they differed from each other as if they belonged to different species. One of them was fat and the other thin. The fat one was full of fun. He worked as if at play. He took a sip of whiskey every now and then, patted the waitress on her behind, and told me to take it easy. He joked with his customers, ate plenty, and enjoyed his food. Working by his side, one could not but be of good cheer. I knew him to be greedy, ruthless, and selfish, but I could not possibly hate him. I kept thinking, Were he to go broke, he would probably be stunned for a while, but his innate joviality would soon assert itself. He would try to recoup his fortune by working for others without bitterness and without a show of servility. He would have his eye on the main chance, take advantage of his fellowmen, and trample them to gain his end, but his spirit and manner would be that of a man disporting himself on a playfield. Should all his efforts fail, he would probably join the migratory workers. He would drink hard and boast of his past glories. His greed might lose its edge. He might share his food and cigarettes with strangers. He would be liked wherever he went.

The thin one ate crackers and milk. He frequently looked into the cash register, turned off the gas, and told me to hurry up. When something went wrong, he looked around to see whether I was nearby and pinned it on me. He preached continually: "All you fellows know is to get your pay." When he paid me off, he counted the money twice and watched my hands lest I cover up a dime. He would finally hand it over to me as if conferring a favor. I thought, Were he to go broke, he would turn into a firebrand revolutionary. He would brew his disappointment into poison and call down damnation on a wicked world. He would walk the streets hollow-eyed, nursing murderous thoughts.

I stayed on in the restaurant several weeks and got to know some of the customers. They called me "Happy" because of my good cheer under all conditions. I helped the waitress during rush hours and found that I liked to serve people. I had the makings of a good servant or valet. One day, the driver who had given me a ride entered the restaurant. We greeted each other and I told him what I had found in the library. I warned him playfully of the sin of misquoting. He brushed it aside. Hope and courage, he said, were the same thing. I did my best to show him the difference. I spoke eloquently and soon several customers joined the discussion. Most of them agreed with me. There is no hope without self-delusion, while courage is sober and sees things as they are. Hope is perishable, while courage is long-lived. It is easy in an outburst of hope to start a difficult undertaking, but it takes courage to bring it to conclusion. It needs courage to win wars, tame continents, build a nation. Man is at his best when his courage enables him to prevail in a hopeless situation.

9

I RETURNED to the road. I cannot remember how long it took me to get to San Diego. In retrospect it seems a lifetime, for it was on this walk that I became an accomplished farmhand. I learned to plow, prune, spray, stack hay, irrigate, and even to graft. I found work in nurseries particularly attractive.

Strangely, this walk so packed with experience left few clear memories behind. Two episodes have remained vivid in my mind. I remember entering one afternoon a small town with a large railroad yard. The town was a center of pea growing and I went there to pick peas. In the morning trucks would roll in to haul the pea pickers to the fields, and I would get on one of them. In the meantime I was lolling on a bench in a small square, watching the happenings around me. There was a bushy tree in the center of the square, its branches touching the ground. I saw a shirt-sleeved arm push through the bushes. The sleeve was stained and dusty but it had a pearl cuff link. The incongruity was startling. Soon a body came in sight: a bedraggled drunk, about my age, with blond hair, unshaven and dirty. Without looking around, he pulled a small mirror from a shirt pocket. He felt his unshaven face as if feeling for damages. I left the square afraid that my presence would embarrass him.

Next morning I saw him standing hesitant and forlorn, as the crowd of pea pickers boarded the trucks. I caught his eye and reached down to help him get on the truck. In the field we took adjoining rows to pick. He was good with his fingers and made as much as I did. When we returned to town in the evening he followed me and rented an adjoining room. We ate in the same restaurant. We were partners, yet we exchanged few words. His name was Bill.

I soon discovered that we were more than partners. The local policeman who knew many of the migratory workers by name complimented me on what I had done for my brother. "He drifted in several weeks ago and did not have a sober day. You could see he was trying to kill himself." Other people also noticed the likeness between us and took it for granted that Bill and I were brothers.

One day we returned from work early. After cleaning up we went out to watch the goings-on in the railroad yard. It was the tourist season and the yard was full of luxury coaches packed with well-dressed people. We could hear snatches of foreign languages. The great world had arrived at our doorstep. We were sitting on a bench close to the wire fence. An engine shunted a coach right across from us. I saw on the back platform a gray-haired man talking animatedly with a young woman. The man was extremely well-dressed and good-looking. The woman was stunningly beautiful. They were two of the most beautiful people I had ever laid eyes on. Still talking, they turned to have a look at the town. I saw the woman grip the man's arm and point excitedly at us across the fence. The engine just then pulled the coach away. I turned to see what Bill's reaction was, but he wasn't there. When I returned to my room the landlady told me that Bill had checked out: "He was in a hurry and left no message."

In the evening, as I came out of the restaurant, the policeman hailed me across the street. "There are people who want to see you," he said, and ushered me into his office. My heart pounded with excitement. There they were—the two beautiful people from the train. They looked eagerly at me.

"Where is Bill?" the man asked. I told him that Bill was gone
and had given up his room, and that I didn't know where he
had gone. Watching his face, I couldn't make out whether the
man believed what I said. But my eyes were now fixed on the
woman's face. I drank in her features. She came over and
took my hand, and as I looked into her deep brown eyes I felt
like one drowning. She said, "If you see Bill, please tell him
that his father and his wife are looking for him, and will go
on looking. We beg him to come home." Her voice is still
lodged in my ears. The man looked at me curiously. "Incredi-
ble," he said. "You could pass for Bill's twin. My name is
Ackerman. We are from Baltimore. The officer has told us
what you have done for Bill. We are terribly grateful. Here is
my card. If you hear from Bill please let us know. And if ever
you come our way please visit us."

They walked out with the officer. The two faces will forever remain fixed in my mind, and I did not allow myself to
speculate on what it was that made Bill run away from home.

The next episode I remember took place in a coastal town
with a large skid row. I arrived in the evening. Next morning
I saw two large trucks roll in. A construction company was
about to build a road in the mountains, and the man in
charge, instead of getting his workers from an employment
agency, sent two trucks to skid row, and anybody who could
get on the truck was hired even if he had only one leg. When
the trucks were full, the drivers put in the tailgates and drove
us east, where they dumped us on the side of a hill. The
company had only one man on the job. We found bundles of
supplies and equipment. Surveyors marked out the road and
we had to build it. I saw something fantastic taking place.
One of us, who had a pencil and a notebook, took down the
names, and we started to sort ourselves out. We had so many
carpenters, blacksmiths, bulldozer and jackhammer men, so

many cooks, first-aid men, and even foremen. We put up the tents, cook shack, toilet, and shower bath, and next morning we went out to build the road. It was an expert job. The rock walls and flumes were works of art. State inspectors hovered around us but could find no fault. The work proceeded automatically. Could a thing like this happen in Russia or anywhere else? I thought, If we had to write a constitution, there would be someone who knew all the *whereases* and *wherefores*. We were a shovelful of slime scooped off the pavement of skid row, yet we could have built America on the side of a hill.

10

$S$AN DIEGO, above the Mexican border, was not only the end of the road but seemed the end of the world. In the early 1930s San Diego was a small, stale town populated by sailors and whores. It did not proclaim itself the best and did not bid me take my chances. There were no jobs. I had to get out before my money was gone. The choice was between retracing my steps northward or crossing 180 miles of desert eastward to the Imperial Valley.

I drifted one evening toward the wholesale produce market. I helped a truck driver unload cabbages from the Imperial Valley, and he promised me a ride to El Centro. We left about midnight, traveling through a moon landscape of peaks and precipices, and it was dawn when the driver dropped me on the outskirts of El Centro. A policeman on a motorcycle caught up with me and directed me to a camp near the railroad yard, where the city gave food and shelter to unemployed migratory workers.

No one could have predicted that my stay in El Centro's transient camp would color all my thinking and would furnish the seed of all I was going to write during the next fifty years. Much has been written about creative milieus which enable an individual to realize and cultivate his talents. Cities like Jerusalem, Athens, Florence of the Renaissance, Amsterdam, Paris, and London were the seedbed of great writers, artists, scientists, and philosophers. Some great universities were centers of creative work. Czarist Russia produced great

novelists and scientists, while Lenin's Russia has been intellec-
tually sterile. At the turn of the eighteenth century, Germany
had been a nursery of great writing and great music, far more
so than imperial Germany. The Orient has been stagnant for
millennia, while the Occident saw a phenomenal flow of creativeness after the end of the Middle Ages. None of the regu-
larities the above facts display and the generalizations they
offer could have shown that a migratory workers' camp in El
Centro would be an ideal milieu for the realization of my
potentialities as thinker and writer.

From the outside the camp looked like a combination of
factory and prison. It was enclosed by a high wire fence, and
inside were three large shacks and a huge boiler topped by a
pillar of black smoke. Men in blue shirts and dungarees were
strolling across the sandy yard. A ship's bell in front of one of
the buildings announced breakfast. The regular members of
the camp ate first, then a crowd of us filed in and were given
a plentiful breakfast. After breakfast I was told that I could
enroll for a stay of several weeks. A brief interview at the
camp office and a physical examination were all the formali-
ties for enrollment.

There were some two hundred men in the camp. They
were the kind I had worked and traveled with since I became
a migratory worker. I even saw familiar faces—men I had
worked with in fields and orchards. Yet my predominant
feeling was one of strangeness. For it is one thing to work and
travel with a crowd and quite another thing to eat, sleep, and
spend the greater part of the day cheek by jowl with two
hundred men. I found myself wondering who these people
around me were. Were they like the people outside? Up to
then I was not aware of the migratory workers as a specific
category of humanity. I knew the people I traveled with as
Americans and Mexicans, whites and blacks, northerners and

southerners. It did not occur to me that they were a group possessed of peculiar traits, and that there was something in their makeup which made them adopt a particular mode of existence.

It was a slight thing that started me on a new track. I got to talking with a mild-looking elderly fellow. I liked his soft speech and pleasant manner. We swapped trivial experiences. Then he suggested a game of checkers. As we started to arrange the pieces on the board, I was startled by the sight of his crippled right hand—half of it was chopped off lengthwise so that the horny stump with its three fingers looked like the leg of a chicken. I was mortified that I had not noticed the crippled hand until he dangled it, so to speak, before my eyes. It was perhaps to bolster my shaken confidence in my powers of observation that I now began paying close attention to the hands of the people around me. The result was astounding. It seemed that every other man had been mangled in some way. There was a man with one arm. Some men limped. One young fellow had a wooden leg. It was as though the majority of the men had escaped the snapping teeth of a machine and left part of themselves behind. It was, I knew, an exaggerated impression, so I began to count cripples as the men lined up in the yard at mealtime. I immediately sensed where the counting would land me. My conclusion preceded the statistical deduction: we in the camp were a human junk pile.

I began to evaluate my fellow tramps as human material, and for the first time in my life I became face-conscious. There were some good faces, particularly among the young. But the damaged and decayed faces were in the majority. I saw faces that were wrinkled or bloated, or raw as the surface of a peeled plum. Some of the noses were purple and swollen, some broken, some pitted with enlarged pores. There were many toothless mouths. My diffidence now vanished. I was getting to know some essential fact about practically everyone. Only seventy of the two hundred were apparently normal.

The connection between our makeup and mode of existence seemed clear. Most of us were misfits. Our contact with a steady job was not unlike a collision. Some of us were maimed, some got frightened and ran away, and some took to drink. There were sixty confirmed drunkards. We inevitably drifted in the direction of least resistance—the open road. We were now in one of the drainage ditches of orderly society. We could not keep our footing in the ranks of the normal and the stable, and were washed into the slough of our present existence. Yet, I mused, there must be in the world a task with an appeal so strong that were we to have a taste of it we would hold on and be rid for good of our restlessness.

My stay in the camp lasted about four weeks. Then I found a haying job not far from town, and finally in April, when the hot winds began to blow, I shouldered my bedroll and took the highway to San Bernardino. It was in the morning, as I walked out of Indio, that a new idea began to take hold of me. The highway out of Indio leads through date groves, grapefruit orchards, and lush alfalfa fields; then, abruptly, it passes into a desert of white sand. The sharp line between garden and desert is very striking. The turning of white sand into garden seemed to me an act of magic. This, I thought, was a job one would jump at—even the men in the transient camp. They had the skill and the ability of the average American. But their energies could be quickened only by a task that was spectacular, that had in it something of the miraculous. The pioneer task of making the desert bloom would fill the bill.

Tramps as pioneers? It seemed absurd. But as I walked on

across the white sand, I kept mulling over the idea. Who were the pioneers? Who were the men who left their homes and went into the wilderness? A man rarely leaves a soft spot and goes deliberately in search of hardship. A man who has made good usually stays put. A change of habitat is usually a painful act of uprooting. Who, then, left for the wilderness and the unknown? Obviously, those who had not made good: men who went broke and never amounted to much; men who, though possessed of abilities, were too impulsive to stand the daily grind; men who were slaves of their appetites—drunkards, gamblers and woman chasers; outcasts—fugitives from justice and ex-jailbirds. Finally, there was a sprinkling of the young and middle-aged in search of adventure. Clearly the same types of people which now swell the ranks of the migratory workers and tramps had probably in former times made up the bulk of the pioneers.

With few exceptions, this seems to have been the case in the settlement of new countries. Ex-convicts were the vanguard in the settling of Australia. Exiles and convicts settled Siberia. In this country, a large portion of our earlier and later settlers were failures, fugitives, and felons. The exception was pioneers motivated by religious fervor.

Somehow this discovery of a family likeness between tramps and pioneers took a firm hold on my mind. For years afterward it kept intertwining itself with a mass of observations which on the surface had no relation to either tramps or pioneers. And it moved me to speculate on subjects in which up to then I had had no real interest. I had stumbled on the seminal problem of the uniqueness of man. In contrast to the patterns which prevail in other forms of life, in the human species the weak not only survive but often triumph over the strong. There is sober realism in St. Paul's stilted words, "God hath chosen the weak things of the world to confound the things which are mighty." The self-hatred inherent in the weak unlocks energies far more formidable than those mobilized by an ordinary struggle for existence. Clearly, the intensity generated in the weak endows them, as it were, with a special fitness. Those like Nietzsche and D. H. Lawrence, who see in the influence of the weak a taint that might lead to decadence and degeneration, are missing the point. It is precisely the peculiar role played by its weak that has given the human species its uniqueness. One should see the dominant role played by the weak in shaping man's fate not as a perversion of natural instincts and vital impulses but as a starting point of the deviation which led man to break away from and rise above nature—not as degeneration but as the generation of a new order of creation.

11

My four-week stay in El Centro's transient camp is the most vividly remembered interval in my life. I remember many faces and even voices. Never before or after has my mind been so lightfooted and fertile. I have gone through life believing that I am at my creative best when alone; actually, most of my seminal ideas were born while I was immersed in a crowd. It is true that I wrote my first and best book in almost total isolation. But the ideas elaborated in the book did not originate in isolation.

My flow of language while in the camp was phenomenal. People were gathering around me whenever I opened my mouth. I discovered that I could turn even trivial experiences into spellbinding stories. I also discovered a gift for rhyming. There was in the camp an ex-sailor by the name of O'Brien, who bragged about his success with women in all parts of the world. My verse "The Importance of Being Named O'Brien" has become part of California's folklore.

> I met girls aplenty
> East and West.
> Some weren't much,
> Some were the best.
> I had them all
> Without even tryin'
> Just because
> My name is O'Brien.

With Mexican señoritas
I am a caballero.
I am OBREGON,
A fighter, a hero.
They give all they have
And sure it's plenty.
My name reminds them
Of El Presidente.

To the ladies of France
I wave my hand
And present myself
As Monsieur OBRIAND,
I get all I want
And I don't have to wait.
My name reminds them
Of a Secretary of State.

With the ladies of Poland
I have all the luck.
I sure have the looks
Of a real Polack.
She tells me her name
Is Anna Rosinsky.
I tell her mine
Is Joseph OBRINSKY.

In Russia the ladies
Are buxom and tough.
They can grab you and lift you
And break you in half.
But with me they are gentle,
So loving and coy,

For I am OBRANOVICH,
The real McCoy.

The director of the camp thought we should put on a
vaudeville show, and I put together a wonderful one, with
songs, dances, and hilarious skits, in almost no time. I still
remember the words and music of much of it. There was one
skit in which a bosomy woman was serenaded by a man with
a guitar, the words set to lilting Italian music.

You are the flower
I am the bee.
You are the cup
I am the tea.
Mine is the labor
Yours is the fee.
Yours is the power
Mine is the plea.

I am the diver
You are the sea.
I am the climber
You are the tree.
Mine is the labor
Yours is the fee.
Yours is the power
Mine is the plea.

Another featured number was a hilarious lecture by a German professor on the origins of the hobo.

I did all the show without assistance from anyone, and all
the time my head was buzzing with new trains of thought. I
was also learning to write. And yet, it did not enter my mind

to capitalize on the new talents and skills. I did not look for a new career that would enable me to live off the fat of the land and also make it possible for me to make the new talents shine in use.

Inwardly, I was a new man when I left the camp. But outwardly I remained one of the army of drifters who followed the crops from one end of California to the other. I was probably a happier man: the preoccupation with the unique role of the misfits in human affairs caused me to compose sentences in the back of my mind even as I was doing my work in the fields and talking with the people around me. Life seemed glorious.

12

My FIRST STAY in the Imperial Valley was the beginning of my full life as a migratory worker. Here began my freight-riding life from one end of California to another, and the establishment of a routine as repetitive and monotonous as the steadiest job one could think of. Beginning with sugar beet thinning in the spring, I followed the unalterable cycle of fruit and vegetable harvesting until I saved enough for a grubstake for prospecting from July to October. The spongy lump of gold (button), when sold in Sacramento, made it possible for me to spend four months of reading, writing, and studying. I have no vivid memories of a gold prospector's adventurous existence. Whatever memories I have of that life have little to do with gold. I never hit it rich. The four months of gold-washing were a monotonous succession of long days of hard work. Whatever vivid memories I have concern my encounters with people. In retrospect, my existence as thinker and writer had more surprises than my life as a prospector.

The most vivid memory of my life as a prospector concerns Phil Hartwick, who raised pears, apples, and potatoes in a canyon north of Placerville. I had bad luck with pay-dirt sluicing and ran out of money early in the season. I remember very clearly how one Sunday morning on the highway between Camino and Placerville a pickup truck, driven by a farmer in blue overalls, pulled up beside me. He had a single oil drum in the back of the truck. Was I looking for work? I told him I was broke.

"Did you ever spray pears?"

"No."

"You are just the man I want. I want someone who has never sprayed pear trees so he'll do exactly what I tell him."

It turned out he was a Seventh Day Adventist. He worked on Sunday and ate no meat. He ate mealies boiled in milk. His dog, tied to a tree in the yard, also lived on boiled mealies and stewed apples.

I had to eat with the farmer until my first pay. I noticed at once his peculiar way of eating. He would take one spoonful and immediately lick the dish. By the time he took the last spoonful the dish was washed clean. When we finished our meal the first evening he told me to take a dish of mealies to the dog. Though I brought him food, the dog bared his yellow teeth and snarled menacingly at me. I put the dish on the ground and kicked it toward him. I watched him swallow the boiled mealies and had the surprise of my life. The dog, after swallowing the first mouthful, did not go on to the next but, like his master, scraped and licked the dish. By the time he was through the dish was washed clean. I wondered whether the dog, like his master, would not eat meat. I hesitated to ask the farmer, but one day when the farmer had to spend the night in Sacramento I had a chance to find out. Incredibly, the dog would not touch the fried bacon I put under his nose. I had to give him mealies and stewed apples. I still wonder how the conversion of the dog was brought about. It was like finding a Jewish dog that wouldn't eat pork. The interaction between a man and his dog is one of life's mysteries.

13

EARLY one summer morning during the prune-picking season I came to the small sleepy town of Healdsburg. I looked for someone to direct me to the large prune orchard of which I had heard, but there was no one in sight. I rested my bedroll on a bench in the small square. Soon an old man with a bushy white beard came over and I questioned him. He answered in broken English, "You no want picking prunes. Hard, dirty work. I give you a job here in the prune yard. Wash prunes. Easy work, good pay."

He led me to a yard on the outskirts of the town where a group of Italians was getting ready for the day's work. They were dumping lugs of prunes into a lye bath, then they spread them out on trays to dry in the sun. My partner, a slim Italian with mischievous eyes and a twirled mustache, was spotlessly dressed in a new khaki shirt. I kept on my peacoat, since the air was still chilly. The trays weighed about a hundred pounds, and we stacked them eighteen high on a trolley. I began to sweat and took off my peacoat. It was not hard work but steady, with no time to catch one's breath. I soon took off my shirt. The day ahead seemed like an endless steep climb. Would I be able to keep up? I looked at my partner, and he seemed cool as a cucumber. Not a stain of sweat on the new shirt. He worked as if at play.

Soon I noticed something curious going on around me. Everybody seemed to watch me, and they were signaling with their fingers the way brokers signal on the stock market.

They were laughing and talking a mile a minute. My partner was humming a song and winking at his fellow Italians. Whatever was going on had to do with me, and I felt that if confidence in my mental capacity was justified I ought to be able to figure out what it was. I watched my partner closely. Why did he find the work so easy? He was half my size and I was the stronger of the two. Suddenly I felt a surge of joy. I got it! Watching him grip the tray, I saw that instead of pulling it toward his chest he put his thumbs under it and pushed it toward me. God had delivered him into my hands. He did not know what was coming. When I next pushed the tray with all my might against him, he staggered backward and the wet prunes cascaded all over him. His new shirt was a mess and the crew's laughter shook the rafters. My partner was cussing something awful, trying to clean himself of the mess. I rushed over to help him and apologized profusely.

We returned to work. My partner was shirtless, while I put on my shirt. Little by little it dawned on me how ominous was the nature of the drama enacted before my eyes. A group of Italian immigrants, probably interrelated and coming from the same part of Italy, had settled around Healdsburg, where they lived a leisurely, prosperous life. They owned their houses and plots of land on which they raised fruits, vegetables, chickens, and milk cows. They made their own wine. In the summer they earned extra money in the prune yards. It was as satisfactory an existence as one could wish for. But it was monotonous. There were very few drunkards. So they invented for themselves an exquisite source of excitement. Each day during the prune-washing season they brought in a stranger, usually a hobo, and put him to work on piling trays. Everybody bet on how long it would take to break the stranger's spirit. They had an elaborate system of betting and large sums of money changed hands.

The fact that I went through the ordeal unbroken marked me as a special person. People shook my hand and patted me on the back. At noon I was stuffed with Italian food and in the evening I discovered that they had a room and a meal ticket at a restaurant to tide me over till payday. They made me one of their family. The outpouring of goodwill and friendship was such that I could not make myself see the repulsive spectacle of breaking the spirit of a defenseless human being before a jeering crowd as an instance of degradation.

14

I N the course of my self-education, I kept for some reason shy of zoology and botany. I mastered textbooks on chemistry, physics, mineralogy, mathematics, and geography, but the animals and plants around me seemed too intricate and mysterious for precise scientific study. However, a slight occurrence eventually plunged me into a passionate preoccupation with botany.

I spent several weeks each year in a plant nursery at Niles. I enjoyed the humid air in the glasshouses, heavy-laden with the scent of growth. One year I spent the whole time transplanting tomato seedlings to cardboard pots. It was tedious work and I did not think I could endure it for long. Then one afternoon, as I was disentangling the rootlets of a seedling from the moss, I began to wonder why the roots of the seedling grew downward and its stem upward! It was an awesomely simple question, like Why do I breathe or sleep? I was certain that someone had already asked the question and found the answer. Any textbook on botany would give me the information. But I wanted to know the answer right away, without delay. I went to the office and asked them for my pay, then caught a freight train to nearby San Jose.

There were several textbooks on botany in the library. I picked the thickest volume, which was Strassburger's textbook, translated from the German. I got a room and a dishwashing job and started to read.

I found the reading difficult. The sentences were packed

with Latin and Greek terms. Dictionaries were no help. I was ready to give up, when wild chance put an end to my troubles. I stopped one day to browse in a tray of secondhand books in a bookstore near the library. I picked up a slender volume bound in cheap wrapping paper. It was a German dictionary of botanical terms, prepared by a Professor Muehe, who taught botany at the agricultural college in Berlin. It was thorough and never failed me. It gave the meaning and etymology of each term. In addition, there were thumbnail biographies of outstanding botanists and a description of famous botanical institutes. I became attached to the booklet. I cherished it as I would a magic oracle that knows all the answers. When my passionate preoccupation came to an end, I still kept the booklet in my knapsack. Years later I parted from it, and the parting was dramatic. It happened on top of a freight train. I was absorbed in working out a difficult line of thought that had nothing to do with botany and I came up against what seemed an insurmountable obstacle. I knew it would take much hard thinking to solve my problem. Then I saw my hand reach out automatically to fish Muehe's oracle out of the knapsack. In a flash I realized that I would probably avoid hard thinking if I had someone always at my side who knew the answers. I was not, in that case, a natural thinker. It was an unpleasant discovery, which I refused to accept. I flung the booklet into the wind.

Unlike other categories of science, botany kept its hold on me even after I was through with Strassburger's textbook. I had a vivid awareness of what was going on inside a plant and felt I could advise farmers when they had trouble with their crops. At one time my interest in botany offered me entrance into an attractive new career.

Although gold-washing gave me enough to keep me going until harvest time, I spent the winters in Berkeley, where I earned some extra money as a part-time busboy. It was thus I met Professor Stilton. I was clearing the tables of empty dishes one day, when I saw a tall, elderly man bent over two thick books opened side by side. I heard him mutter under his breath in exasperation, and I asked him playfully whether there was something I could do for him. He looked up, startled, but seeing me he smiled. He was reading a German book on leaf-yellowing. The other thick book was a German-English dictionary. "The German language," he exploded, "was the devil's own invention. I have been trying for hours to get the meaning of just one sentence, which begins at the top of one page and ends at the bottom of the next. By the time I reach the end I forget the beginning. It so happens that this monstrous sentence contains vital information, and I need to know its precise meaning. The dictionary is not of much help." I told him that I knew German and would be glad to try my hand translating the sentence. The professor, laughing, pushed over the book, paper, and a pencil, and I easily bucked the German log into stove-sized pieces. He looked incredibly at my handiwork. Then, laughing again, he spoke with amazing frankness.

He was, he told me, the head of the citrus department at the University of California. At the moment the department was engaged in the investigation of a disease which had recently made its appearance in the lemon-growing districts of southern California. The leaves of the trees mottled, then yellowed, and finally dropped. The repeated defoliation had drastically reduced the lemon crop. His department was doing good work. But it would be fitting if he, as the head of the department, prepared a survey of the literature dealing with leaf chlorosis in general. The literature was vast and most of it in German. Would I consider working for his department? I would be hired as a nursery man in one of the hothouses, but my real work would be translating from the German. I jumped at his offer. I was determined not only to do the translating but also to immerse myself in the literature on chlorosis and perhaps hit upon a solution. I had faith in my originality. I told him of my botanical studies. It was thus I became a member of a university department.

I tried to learn what the department had already accomplished. It turned out that both the lemon growers and the botanists believed that chlorosis was due to a shortage of water. And since the trees were getting all the water they possibly needed, it was assumed that some poisonous impurity in the copious commercial fertilizer was damaging the root system. The thing to do therefore was to leach the soil around the trees thoroughly. But, so far, leaching had not proved to be a cure. Then, by a chance as wild as the one that landed Muehe's dictionary in my lap, I hit upon a solution. I remembered reading that even a minute amount of boron in the soil could cause chlorosis. I now jumped to the conclusion that if the nitrate fertilizer was given in the form of calcium nitrate rather than sodium nitrate the calcium would combine with boron in an insoluble compound and thus neutralize its damaging effect on the roots.

In my enthusiasm I rushed to the professor to tell him about my hunch. Jokingly, I added, "Please wire one of the large lemon growers to use calcium nitrate and see what happens."

He laughed and looked at me curiously. "You know," he said, "I'll do just that," and immediately sent off a wire.

It took some days before we got the results. Then one day Dr. Stilton burst upon me, smiling broadly, and threw his arms around me. "It worked!" he shouted. "We have licked chlorosis."

He was ready to give me his department. But I knew instinctively that my time for settling down had not yet arrived. I returned to the open road.

ALTHOUGH migratory workers live and travel in packs, their slogan is "Everybody for himself," as much as it is with businessmen. It is rare for migratory workers to form enduring friendships, and least of all to pool their earnings. I had such a rare experience for a time, but it needed a fantastic combination of circumstances to bring this about. It was my discovery of the essays of Montaigne that made this possible.

My self-education progressed most markedly when I was placer mining. I had time to study, think, and even learn to write. One year, as I was to go up to the mountains, I had a hunch that I would be snowbound and I had to provide myself with enough reading material to keep me going during the workless days. I decided to buy a thick book of about a thousand pages. It mattered not what the book was about so long as it was thick and had small print and no pictures. I found such a book in a secondhand bookstore and bought it for one dollar. It was only after I bought it that I turned to the title page. It said that these were the *Essays of Michel de Montaigne*. I knew what essays were but nothing of Montaigne.

My hunch about the snow was right, and I read the Montaigne book three times until I almost knew it by heart. Here was a book written by a French nobleman hundreds of years ago about himself, yet I felt all the time that he was writing about me. I recognized myself on every page. He knew my innermost thoughts. The language of the book was precise, almost aphoristic. I discovered the charms of a good sentence. When I got back to the San Joaquin Valley I could not open my mouth without quoting Montaigne, and the fellows liked it. It got so that whenever there was an argument about anything—women, money, animals, food, death—they would ask, "What does Montaigne say?" Out came the book, and I would find the right passage. I would not be surprised if even now there are migratory workers up and down the San Joaquin Valley still quoting Montaigne. One little Italian in particular, by the name of Mario, hung on my lips whenever I quoted Montaigne. Once he asked me bashfully to read him some passages from the book. We were picking cotton and lived out in the open, and one evening, as I rushed to the store to buy something to eat, he pulled my sleeve and shook his head. "This no good. I cook good food. You come eat with me." He had some sort of a stove and in no time served me a meal I could never forget.

Thus evening after evening I bought the makings of a meal and he cooked it. I felt guilty that he should have to cook after a hard day's work, so one day I said to him, "Mario, you and I are partners. From now on you stop work at noon every day and go to cook while I will work the rest of the day. We will divide the pay." Thus began for me a period of luxury eating. He got hold of delicacies from Italian farmers in the neighborhood and we had wine, brandy, and even cigars. He made of the evening meal a festive occasion. He made a table of an orange crate and used a clean towel as a table cover. He ate by himself before I returned from work and served me as a waiter would serve clients in a restaurant. After the meal, lighting a cigar and sipping brandy, I was expected to discourse. I talked about Montaigne, about Italy's role in creating Western civilization, about the uniqueness of America, and the like. All the time I had the feeling that he was trying to re-create a tableau which had impressed itself upon his mind as a child. In a poor Italian village the style of life of the rich landowner was a matter of absorbing curiosity. I could see little Mario peering through the fence into a garden where the rich man and his friends were feasting at a table, sipping brandy, smoking cigars, and discoursing.

Mario excelled particularly in the cooking of vegetables. How beautiful are the vegetables displayed in our markets and of what astounding variety! Pyramids of shining tomatoes, rows of eggplant with a luster of dark enamel and the mystery of sleeping beauties, patches of radishes bordered with feathery parsley, pods of green peas stacked like sacks, heaps of shiny bell peppers—a riot of colors and shapes. But cooking turns all this glory into a shapeless, colorless, and often tasteless mass. Slapped on a dish, the vegetables look like dead corpses and taste all alike. Mario cooked vegetables so as to bring out their particular flavor and aroma. He performed wonders with eggplants and cauliflower. He peeled the eggplant and cut it lengthwise into thin slabs. He let the slabs dry in the sun for an hour, then fried them in olive oil until deep brown. He then placed the browned slabs into a pot, covered them with water, added pieces of bell pepper and a tooth of garlic and stewed them until they turned black. By the time he was through, eggplant tasted like sautéed mushrooms. His cooking of cauliflower was a work of art. He split a head of cauliflower into medium-sized branches, dipped each branch in egg and fried them until brown. He transferred the fried branches to a pot, sprinkled them with salt, added a tooth of garlic, covered them with a cup of strong lemonade, and cooked them until the golden stew thickened. The golden end product had the smell of flowers and filled the eater's mouth with a symphony of flavors.

We went on like this for weeks. This was in 1936. One evening I spoke of Mussolini. I wondered why the noble Italian nation allowed a vulgar, empty-headed charlatan to kick them around. I sensed immediately that something awful had happened. Mario's face froze. He got up, took his things, and walked away. He never spoke to me again.

16

To a migratory worker the hop-picking season is an oasis of human warmth. Picking the papery berries from suspended vines is clean and easy work. One can work and talk with people in adjoining rows, swap stories and jokes at the same time. The people who pick hops come from all walks of life. There are no professional pickers. Retired businessmen, social servants and craftsmen, students and housewives with their children do most of the picking. There is warm camaraderie. They live together out in the open, cook and sleep under a starlit sky, sing and dance.

I spent the hop-picking season in Mrs. Trenton's yard near Santa Rosa. Mrs. Trenton, her husband, and three tall sons welcomed me as an old acquaintance. The strange story of how Mrs. Trenton came to marry Mr. Trenton made big-breasted, plain-looking Mrs. Trenton for me a source of great curiosity. She was a great beauty as a girl and belonged to a well-to-do family in Santa Rosa. Mr. Trenton was a common mule skinner, a ruffian and a drunkard. One day, as he drove through Santa Rosa, he caught a glimpse of a girl and felt like one struck by lightning. He abandoned his wagon and began running around asking about the girl. When he learned who she was he started drinking and went around telling people that he was the dirtiest dirt. In a sober interval he went to the girl's house, got down on his knees and told her that, although he was the plainest dirt, he would not go on living unless she became his wife. So she married him and ruled him with an iron rod. She did not bring him a penny, but made him toil and save, and in fifty years they piled up a fortune.

I usually parked my bedroll near Mrs. Bruner's trailer. Mrs. Bruner treated me as a relative and wanted me to settle in Auburn, in the gold country, and marry her niece. Mr. Bruner, a retired civil servant, was full of fun and delighted in inventing fairy tales with a California background. I always wondered whether these marvelous tales would be remembered when Mr. Bruner was gone. One tale in particular impressed itself upon my mind. It concerned Johnny the bum, who was famous up and down the land for his ability to bamboozle people into feeding him without his ever doing a lick of work. One day, as he was riding on top of a freight train in northern California, he was overcome with hunger. Normally he would get off the train and walk over to the nearest farm with the certainty of being fed. But in this part of the country the only farm in sight was that of the widow Jones, and she was known up and down the land for never feeding a bum unless he chopped wood. He had no choice. As he entered the farmyard he heard the farm animals laughing: "Look who is coming." The dog was jumping with joy. Johnny knocked on the door and there was widow Jones, ax in hand. She had seen him coming through the window. She pointed to a clump of trees not far from the house and said, "Here is the ax. Cut down the trees into firewood and I'll feed you." Johnny shouldered the ax and, followed by the dog, walked over toward the trees. As he neared the clump he heard the trees laughing, saying to each other; "Look at Johnny with the ax. Is it not sidesplitting?" The word "sidesplitting" made Johnny pause. He knew that God was with him. He was going to tell the trees a joke so funny that the laughter would split their sides and all he'd have to do would be to gather the pieces. Johnny sat down under a tree and started to tell a story about a Chinese woodcutter. During the gold-rush days many Chinese came to California. They were not allowed to mine gold-rich dirt but had to get what gold they could by washing the tailings of white miners. When they ran out of tailings one Chinaman decided to become a woodcutter. He got himself an ax and knocked on a door. A woman opened the door and said, "Yes?"

The Chinaman said, "Me cut wood."

The woman said, "How much?"

He said, "Cut, chop, stack, three dollars a cord."

"Oh," said the woman, "that is very nice. How much cut, chop, no stack?"

The Chinaman counted on his fingers and said, "Two dollars, seventy cents."

The woman smiled. "How much cut, no chop, no stack?"

The Chinaman again figured with his fingers. "Two dollars a cord."

"Wonderful," said the woman. "How much no cut, no chop, no stack?"

The Chinaman again worked his fingers and looked confused. He started again to count on his fingers and finally burst out, "You clazy."

The trees shook with mirth so violently that they split their sides. Johnny gathered the pieces into a bundle and started to walk back to the farm. He noticed that one tree was left standing. He asked the dog; "What's the matter with this tree?"

"Oh," said the dog, "this is an English walnut tree."

Johnny shook his head and resumed his walk. About a hundred yards farther he heard a big noise behind him. He turned to look: the English walnut tree was splitting its sides.

17

The winter months in Berkeley were richer in human encounters than the months of harvesting and placer mining. In many ways, Berkeley resembled the fabulous transient camp in El Centro. There was in both a creative ferment and tension. When trying to explain the surprising resemblance, one hits upon the role of the small city as a creative milieu. Civilization was born in the small cities of Sumer and evolved in the small cities of Jerusalem, Athens, Florence, and Amsterdam. It is the individual who creates. In a creative milieu the individual is conscious of his identity but also has living ties with a communal entity. In a village the individual is swallowed in the communal body, while in a big city the distinct individual finds it hard to form communal ties. Hence in both village and big city there is a paucity of human encounters. Both Berkeley and the transient camp had the virtues of a small city.

In Berkeley human encounters often opened a door to the possibility of a new life. I have told of my encounter with Dr. Stilton, which opened the door to an academic career. Another encounter which has left a deep imprint on my mind was with Edward Mohl. I was working as a busboy in a cafeteria on Shattuck Avenue. The cafeteria was open twenty-four hours, and I happened to work the graveyard shift. One day, toward dawn, a startling figure entered the cafeteria. I was struck by his distinguished appearance and air of authority. He was good-looking and extremely well dressed. Not only were his clothes tailor-made and of the finest material, but you knew that much thought went into choosing each item of apparel. He probably took more care in choosing a tie than one of our sort takes in choosing a wife. He ordered a cup of coffee and sat down at a table. He was not the kind who ate in cafeterias, but it was too early for restaurants to open. As he pulled up his pant leg I was appalled by the sight of a hole in one of the socks. I knew that if I did not do something about it, I would be worried all day long. Clearly, from the way he was dressed he was on his way to some important meeting. The sight of a hole in the sock might prove disastrous. I rushed down to the basement, got a needle and thread of the right color, and went over to his table. He looked up, startled, and fixed me with his deep-blue eyes. I told him about the hole and asked him to let me have the sock. He laughed uproariously, took off the sock, and watched me mend the hole. When I had finished, he fished a twenty-dollar bill out of his wallet and offered it to me. I refused to take it, telling him that I had to do what I did to preserve my peace of mind. He introduced himself, asked for my name, and we shook hands. Next morning he arrived at the same time and handed me a beautiful gold watch. It was inscribed, "To Eric Hoffer for his thoughtfulness from E.M." I thanked him warmly and we chatted for some time. I never heard who he was and never saw him again, but the memory of him is still vivid in my mind after thirty-some years.

Of course, my most memorable encounter was with Helen. One early summer morning, as I was leaving the restaurant, I saw the red train pull up on Shattuck Avenue. I wondered what sort of people were traveling on a train so early. I saw two women get off. They had a small suitcase. They stood there looking around them, obviously strangers. I was suddenly seized with an impulse to speak to them. I walked over, almost running. I said, "Can I be of service to you?"

They looked startled. The two were as different from each other as day and night. One was tall and of striking beauty, the other squat and ugly.

"Are you the baggage man?" asked the ugly one.

I said, "No, I am a busboy."

We all laughed. I covered my embarrassment by talking a mile a minute. Were they students? It was vacation time at the university, and the next semester was months ahead. Were they perhaps to attend summer school? They'd need time to settle down. Anyhow, the most important thing right then was breakfast. I took their suitcase and they followed me to the restaurant, laughing. I picked a table and then went over to the counter and ordered orange juice, fruit, and ham and eggs. They kept laughing as they ate and looked at me curiously.

I sensed a stirring of suspicion in the eyes of the ugly one. I said, "Please don't be alarmed. I am not a madman and it is not my habit to accost strangers and buy them breakfast. When I saw you get off the train I was seized with a sudden impulse to rush over and speak to you. Such impulses are rare, but when they come I have learned not to resist them. I feel touched by the finger of fate. You need someone to help you find living quarters and get your luggage. I work nights and am free during the daytime. I know of a place you might want to rent. It stands on a hill off Euclid Avenue. I know the owner, Mr. Parker, and I am sure the rent will be reasonable."

I got a taxicab and we drove up to Mr. Parker's house. He was delighted to have the girls for tenants, and they loved the house, which had a wonderful view of the bay. Before leaving them, I asked for the baggage ticket and brought up their things and an armful of flowers. They stood looking open-mouthed as I bid them good-bye. The name of the beautiful one was Helen.

18

I T WAS past midnight, about a week after my encounter
with the girls, when I saw Helen enter the cafeteria. I rushed
to meet her. She threw her arms around me and kissed me.
Holding hands, we walked over to a table. We looked at each
other in silence. Her brown eyes were so deep that my heart
pounded with fear. I felt fate brush against me. It had
brought me a gift beyond compare. Did I deserve it? I knew
that from that moment I would be a different person. No
matter where I would go and where I might end up, this
incredibly sweet face would be with me. Even now, fifty
years later, I see her so alive that I am prompted to reach out
and touch her.

"Why didn't you come up to the house?" she asked.

I said, "I was afraid I might seem a pushy busboy."

She shook her head. "What does it matter what you do?
You are a dear, rare human being. We have been telling
everybody about you. Please be our friend. Come up in the
evening. Fred will cook a fine meal and we shall be together.
She is an excellent cook."

The cafeteria was almost empty. We sat there holding
hands and looking at each other in wonder. She saw the book
at my elbow and asked what I was reading. I told her about
Dostoevski's *The Idiot* and how it came about that I was
rereading the book every year. Her eyes were sparkling with
mirth.

It was time for her to go home, I thought. Berkeley had

only one cab at this hour, but luckily the cab station was right across the street and the driver was there. I helped her get into the cab and paid the driver. She kissed me as they drove off.

I stood there, deeply moved. Did it actually happen? The most beautiful and precious woman in the world came past midnight to tell me that she loved me. I had no sense of inferiority but not even in my wildest dream would I have imagined a beautiful woman falling on my shoulder, hugging and kissing me, and telling me she loved me. I could never believe that I was an exceptional person. Sooner or later I would be cut down to size.

I went up to the Parker house in the evening. The girls welcomed me warmly. Fred returned to the kitchen while Helen and I stood by the window looking at the shimmering bay. She had her arm around my waist. Soon Fred joined us. She was wiping her hands with her apron as she said, "We still don't know what made you speak to us. It was so funny and wonderful." I told them of my encounter with Edward Mohl and the hole in his sock. I showed them the gold watch. They shook with laughter.

I helped Helen set the table for a meal of meatloaf, Burgundy wine, and fresh Italian bread. I ate my fill. Fred kept asking searching questions, wanting to know about my life. I told them about the yearly routine of harvesting, placer mining, and winters in Berkeley. The fact that I was mining gold surprised them no end. By chance I had a phial of gold dust with me. They looked at it in wonder and I told them to keep it. It was ten o'clock when I left.

I went up to the house every evening after that, and it soon seemed as if the three of us had always been together. The evenings assumed a pattern. After dinner we would have tea, and I was expected to talk about the things that had happened to me from as far back as I could remember. I told stories, some of which sounded like fairy tales, and the girls listened with eyes shining, like children. As I later found out, they memorized every detail. Watching them as they exchanged glances from time to time, I could see that my stories confirmed the exaggerated opinion they had of me. I must write the stories down, Helen insisted. She was wonderfully excited.

Helen was an impulsive person, as I already knew, and tenderhearted. She also had unexpected moods of playfulness and would occasionally invite a bout of wrestling. With her youthful strength and considerable skill, there were times when she could get me to the floor on my back.

Her tenderheartedness was extended to all of God's creatures. I remember in particular one day when Mr. Parker hired me to clear the weeds around the house and Helen insisted on helping with the job. An immediate difficulty revealed itself. As we set about turning the soil, we discovered the ground teeming with life. Every turn of the shovel uncovered lizardly water dogs with brown backs, orange bellies, and green eyes. There were also regular lizards, stiff and dazed, spiders, potato bugs, centipedes—both brown and blue—crablike scorpions, earthworms, and here and there a small snake or a field mouse with its nest of downy straw. Helen said firmly that we must not kill any of these creatures, and I agreed. By working the soil with a pick I managed to split it in large clods which Helen then broke carefully, rescuing the living hosts. They were just coming to life, she said, and had a summer of feeding, mating, and breeding ahead. By gathering them into a basket she transferred them to an acacia thicket at the back of the house. Only the spiders and potato bugs were brisk enough to run. I handled the scorpions and centipedes myself. Were they poisonous? We didn't know. So Helen went down to the campus for information, to be told that the California centipedes were harmless, the scorpions poisonous. What to do with them? Kill them? It is not so much the death of a scorpion that is unsettling to watch, but the pain and writhing before it dies. We both hit upon the same solution: an anaesthetic. It was only necessary to acquire a bottle of chloroform, spoon the scorpions into a bottle containing a piece of gauze soaked in the liquid, screw the cover tight, and the deed was done. The scorpions showed no fight.

By this time it was dark and we were ready to go into the house and wash up for dinner.

In time Helen enrolled at Bolt Hall for graduate work. Now and then I met her on the campus and we had lunch in one of the cafeterias. She made many friends. One day she told me that people in the mathematics and physics department thought it would be possible for me to audit classes in higher mathematics and advanced physics. She was told that surprising discoveries were recently made in both departments and several Nobel prizes were won. I kept silent. She said, "It would be wonderful if you could spend a whole year with us in Berkeley. Later, if you feel like it, you could return to harvesting and mining. We have been so happy these months."

The girls had a plan. Fred lectured me one evening about a goal. People must feel that they are going somewhere. It was a sin to waste my great talents. Helen had told her about the new physics. With my gift for theorizing I could do wonders. She was sure I could do better than any man in the physics department. With my extraordinary capacity for mathematics I might become another Einstein.

It made no sense. The two women had made up their minds that it was their duty to make me a wonderman. It was sheer madness. I loved Helen dearly. But it would be miserable to spend my few remaining years trying to justify their expectations. The people in the physics department would soon think me a fraud. I did not believe a word about my exceptional talents. If I lived with the girls I would not have a moment's peace. I had to act immediately, and decided to return to the road. When harvest time approached I left Berkeley without taking leave of the girls.

19

IT TOOK me years to recover from my break with the girls. Actually, I never wholly recovered. Not only did I feel as if my mind had been torn apart, but my body lost its balance. I broke out with boils and my eyes dimmed. I had to buy glasses. I avoided Berkeley and instead spent my winters in Sacramento. For the first time in my life I knew loneliness. People who feel lost and abandoned lose track of their comings and goings. They have no history. I have only a pale memory of that period. I remember being befriended by Jeany, a warm-hearted prostitute. I obviously had a need to attach myself to somebody. I was no longer self-sufficient and aloof. There was also a change in my routine of harvesting. I worked for the first time in cotton fields and on the railroad.

I met Jeany in Jack's Restaurant. I had just come down from the hills, where for four months I hardly saw a human being. Jeany had a seat opposite me, and she smiled. I started to talk about gold mining, showing her a phial of gold dust, which I usually carried around with me. She invited me to her apartment and we made love. When she told me how she earned a living I wanted to pay her but she refused, so I gave her the phial of gold. I saw Jeany often, took her out to eat and to the movies. It was a restful relationship. I remember a funny incident. I had a cheap watch to which I was attached because it kept perfect time. One day, after a visit to Jeany, I missed the watch and returned to her place to see whether she had found it. It amused me to see the watch hanging on the wall next to the bed. I thought it was a fitting place for an old watch to spend its old age and left it where it was.

It was in a cotton field near Fresno that I first saw George Anseley. The cotton was such as pickers pray for: stalks of medium height, and clusters of large balls offering their cotton with overflowing generosity. You simply waved your hands in the manner of a magician and the cotton was in your sack. I noticed the picker in the row to my right. He did not seem in a hurry, yet I found it difficult to keep up with him. His hands moved with a wonderful rhythm, fast and without a lost motion. His face did not have a trace of the birdlike sharpness which settles on a fast picker in action. I had to pick as I never picked before to keep up with him. The pace continued for almost two hours. We finished our rows almost simultaneously. I doubt whether during the two hours of what I considered a breath-taking race he was in the least aware of me. We dropped down on our bulging sacks and he smiled. His smile impressed me as something bright and new, something usually concealed in the velvet of his eyes and rarely displayed. I produced my package of cigarettes and he his. I offered him one and he offered me one. We both struck matches. I lighted his cigarette and he lighted mine. All the time his smile lingered on his face.

For weeks we continued to work side by side without exchanging a word. I knew his name because it was called out by the farmer when he weighed our sacks. He gave no sign that he accepted me as a companion or knew my name, but I knew beyond doubt that he was infinitely superior to myself. To be at his side seemed a distinction. When someone referred to Anseley as my partner I was pleased no end.

Here is perhaps how it was. The earth is teeming with human beings. You see them in towns, in fields, and on the roads, but you rarely notice them. And then your eyes meet a face and you are struck with wonderment. You are suddenly aware of the sublime uniqueness of the human race, unlike anything on earth. "In His own image He made him." There is a great lonesomeness about such an encounter, as of something that came from another planet.

Anseley had one habit which was to me a source of fear and worry. When out in the fields and not working he would spread out his cotton sack or his coat and stretch out on his back, dead. He would remain in the same position for hours, without showing a sign of animation. Seeing him thus, I could not be certain that he would come to life again.

One day a contractor hauled the crew out to do some first picking at ninety cents a hundred pounds. Once there, however, he switched us to a large field of second picking and expected us to pick at the same rate of pay. We refused. The contractor, a southern gentleman, harangued us, begging and threatening. Someone in front made fun of him and the contractor lost his temper and jumped him. It ended with the contractor getting a beautiful beating, black eyes and all, and we cheered and danced. Now, through all this hullabaloo Anseley lay on his back, to all appearances dead.

Only once during the first year did I hear Anseley speak. It took place in a cotton field near Hanford. The grower promised us cabins and shower baths, but all we found were tents with dirt floors and one faucet. At the end of one week we were ready to quit. When the payoff started, it appeared that the grower's bookkeeping was somewhat mixed up. Some of the pickers cried out that he had them for less than they had picked. The grower assumed that other pickers were getting more than was coming to them. When he came to Anseley and me, he thought that he had credited us with more than we had earned. I was ready with a flow of words but Anseley was ahead of me. He addressed the grower in a mild, even tone: "Sir! I remember every one of our separate weighings, Eric's and mine. If you don't mind I shall call them out so that you may see whether they tally with your figures." And sure enough, Anseley had all of our weighings in his head, five weighings a day for each of us—sixty numbers all together. Not only did Anseley have a phenomenal memory, but he knew my name and took interest in things which concerned me.

It was inevitable that Anseley should become mixed up in my mind with Helen. They belonged together. I saw them standing side by side, the noblest examples of the human race. I made up my mind to take Anseley to Berkeley and have him meet the girls.

We reached the Bakersfield railroad yard in time to catch the hotshot freight train which rolled through the San Joaquin Valley with hardly any stops until it reached Oakland. The train usually slowed down as it passed through railroad yards. We had often before boarded trains traveling at fifteen miles an hour, but I found it necessary to tell Anseley to grab hold of the iron ladder of a boxcar and climb to the top without minding me. Later we would get together. The train slowed down to about ten miles, and as I climbed a boxcar I could see Anseley a few cars ahead getting to the top. When I reached the top I waved my hand and he waved his. I shouted to him to sit where he was, but my words were drowned by the clatter of the wheels. I saw him jump the gap between two cars. I hurried to meet him. The train was gathering speed rapidly. Anseley's face was aglow with excitement as he ran on top of the shaking car, and I motioned him to sit down, but he decided to come over to me. He was almost within my reach when the speeding train rounded a sharp bend. The cars swerved outward as Anseley jumped. He was flung out and backward. His hands went up clutching the wind. He turned in midair and his back was toward me as I jumped after him. I can still see him floating, his legs pulled in, his arms stretched sideways, and his brown hair curling over the collar of his jacket.

When I opened my eyes I felt as if I had been running miles upon miles to find someone. My breath came in gasps. There was a weight pressing upon my chest, and I closed my eyes in an effort to get out from underneath it. When I opened my eyes again I saw the tired face of a middle-aged nurse.

I said, "How is Anseley?" She said, "You must not speak. Your friend is dead."

20

I CAME out of the hospital weary and dazed. I felt greatly diminished and lacked the zest to resume the routine of harvesting and placer mining. I barely had enough energy to follow the passive, drifting life of a typical migratory worker. Nor was I going to return to Sacramento. Instead, I hitched a ride to Stockton. It was the height of the tomato-picking season, and the sidewalks of Stockton's skid row were packed with tattered fruit pickers waiting for the trucks to haul them out to the fields. The moment the trucks hove into view there was a mad rush to climb aboard, and I was carried along with the crowd. In less than five minutes the trucks were full, and we were driven out to the tomato fields, which stretched to the distant horizon. The rush continued for empty boxes and for good rows of vines. Darkness fell all of a sudden, no one had time to watch the sun in its course. There was another rush to catch the trucks back to town, to line up for pay, and to get supper in the crowded cheap restaurants.

When tomato picking was over I decided to shift to Tracy, which was in closer contact with harvesting. I joined the crowd that was waiting for the Tracy-bound freight. There were about twenty of us. No one talked. I sat leaning on my bundle, staring listlessly ahead of me. Then I saw a little man climb out of a ditch beyond the tracks. He was panting under a heavy pack. He had on gold-rimmed glasses and looked very neat. He smiled at us, he relieved himself of the pack. Still panting, he said, "What a day! So help me, I can't remember where I was yesterday." I scrutinized the shriveled face. It was bluish red with a fine network of reddish veins. A hard drinker, he had probably got drunk the day before in Roseville and stumbled into a boxcar which was hitched to a Stockton-bound freight. A methodical drunk, he had secured his glasses and pack. He noticed my probing eyes and came over to sit beside me. When the train pulled in, we clambered into the same gondola and I helped him with his pack. Soon the train gathered speed. We traveled through level fields covered with deep quilts of alfalfa and spotted with cattle. After crossing a muddy river we reached Tracy.

The little man knew his way about in the railroad yard and motioned me to follow him. As we came out into the street he pointed to a sign ahead of us. It was a saloon, The Stag. We entered a dingy room full of smoke and men drinking. The little man threw off his pack, took off his hat, and walked over to the piano. Soon the room reverberated with the sound of his playing and singing. It was a popular song: "I Know You Are No Angel." I took a chair beside the piano. The little man eyed me with triumph, and with gesticulations as expressive as words told me to take his hat and make the rounds of the house. It was as if it happened in a dream. They gave nickels, and some gave dimes and even quarters. At a table near the door sat a woman. She was the only woman in the saloon. As I approached her she stared at me with haughtiness. My heart began to pound as I searched her beautiful face. The deep black eyes, the small mouth, the nose, and the tiny ears with almost no lobes reminded me of Helen. I rushed back to the piano, gave the hat to the little man, shouldered my bundle, and rushed out of the saloon.

As I came out into the sunshine I saw coming toward me a man with a small satchel strapped to his shoulder. He seemed in high spirits, and I asked him where I might catch a freight

to San Jose. He said, "Come with me and I'll show you. It's in
front of Tom Wing's Restaurant."

The bench in front of the restaurant was occupied by men
with bundles. Waiting there, I soon saw the man with the
satchel come out of the restaurant, followed by the Chinese
owner, his wife, and his children. They were all talking volubly. The satchel was a painter's box, and the Chinaman was
agreeing to pay a dollar for the repainting of the sign. The
deal concluded, the painter scraped off the words "Tom
Wing" with a razor blade, and with beautiful skill painted
the words "Lee's Restaurant" in yellow paint. When the Chinaman protested against the yellow color, the painter assured
him that he would turn the yellow into silver.

In the meantime, a crowd had gathered. It was a historic
event. The painter asked me to roll him a cigarette and, taking it, he said, "Stick to me, brother, and you will never go
hungry." When he finished the painting, he dusted the letters
with a white powder which turned them silver. The crowd
applauded, the Chinaman gave the painter a dollar bill, and
the painter went into the restaurant, soon to come out again
scrubbed and combed. Heading a procession, he walked off
to the nearby wine shop, while I stayed behind.

It was then that I first saw Abner Ward. He was sitting on
the end of the bench, upright and motionless as a statue. His
face was expressionless. He tried to get up but could not make
it. He was dead drunk. Moved by an impulse I could not
resist, I went over and took his arm. I asked where he lived. A
boy who watched us said, "I know," and pointed to a small
shack up the street. It was hard going to get to the shack. I
found the key in Ward's pocket and unlocked the door. I saw
a small room, as neat as anything I had ever seen. I got him to
the bed, took off his boots, and stretched him out on his back.
He lay there, sunk in a deep stupor, while I sat beside the bed

and studied the face. Of the thousands of faces I have seen over a long life, hardly more than a dozen have imprinted themselves on my mind and become part of my inner landscape. The face before me belonged to that category. On the table there were three thick books—the Bible, a Bible commentary, and *The Outline of History* by H. G. Wells.

It was getting dark and I turned on the light. I leafed through the books and watched the bed. Finally Ward began to stir. He turned on his side and looked at me in wonder. I told him how I had helped him get to his shack. He said, "God bless you." He seemed about forty. His strong body still had the slenderness of youth but the weathered face was deeply lined. His gray, mournful eyes brooded under bushy eyebrows and a thatch of bleached hair. Seeing the face, one thought of a man who has been for years on a hopeless errand. His voice was sonorous and his speech unhurried. As he got up from the bed he said, "A man by himself is in bad company." Then he went over to the stove and we were soon sharing a cheese omelet and a green salad. Contrary to what I expected, he talked volubly. The man had apparently been living for a long time in total isolation and now grasped the chance of talking to a sympathetic listener. In retrospect, it seems that he kept talking for weeks, mainly about his life. I shall try to piece together his strange story, and tell of its fantastic ending.

21

ABNER WARD was a God-fearing man. His God was Jehovah, Lord of the open spaces where sheep and cattle graze, and man wrestles with his soul, torn between good and evil. Abner was a sheepherder and a boozer.

Can a man read the Bible and not long for the life of a sheepherder? Abraham, Isaac, Jacob and his twelve sons, Moses, and others were sheepherders. So were some of the prophets: "The words of Amos who was a sheepherder from Tekoa." The kings were shepherds of their people, and God himself is a shepherd: "He feeds His flock, He gathers His lambs in His arms and carries them in His bosom, and gently leads those that are with young." But few of the people spoken of in the Bible were drunkards. Some got drunk occasionally. There was Noah, and Nabal the sheepman from Carmel, and Belshazzar, king of Babylon, and Ahasuerus, king of Persia. The prophets thundered against greed, vanity, adultery, and idolatry, but rarely against drink. Booze was not then the curse it is now.

On his return from France at the conclusion of the First World War, Abner paid a brief visit to his hometown, St. Louis, and then went on to California. He had no thought of gold or golden oranges. From childhood his mind had fixed itself on two things: honey and sheep. But in Sacramento, his first stop in California, no one knew much about honey, while the demand for sheepherders was loud on the blackboards in front of the employment agencies.

So Abner became a sheepherder, and few people took greater delight in their work. He had a deep affinity for animals. His dogs, which he raised from puppyhood, were trained to an accurate and delicate obedience. He talked to them as to fellow humans, and they understood and did all the work.

In over fifteen years of herding sheep Abner made the rounds of many of the larger sheep ranches in California. He stayed, as a rule, one year with an outfit. The yearly shifting was due to his addiction to liquor. This failing was as much part of his natural makeup as were his ways with animals, his skill with tools, and his resourcefulness in difficult circumstances. They were a heritage from his pioneer forebears, who not only cleared land, built houses, barns, and furniture with their own hands, fought Indians, and endured hardships, but also made their own liquor and dipped it out of barrels. When the vicissitudes of time swept the family into the staleness, sterility, and gutter drunkenness of St. Louis, the boy's homesickness for the open spaces, coupled with a vague longing for holiness, was the more poignant, since he knew that it was beyond his attainment. The craving for alcohol was lurking in every particle of his being.

For over fifteen years Abner had put a bound to his passion for drink. He held down his thirst, day after day during the lambing season and during the transfer of the flock to the highland pastures. When he returned to the valley in early fall, he called for his pay and boarded a freight. He usually dropped at the first stop, rented a shack, and spent his days drinking, eating, and sleeping. When his money gave out, he directed himself to the nearest sheep ranch and resumed another year of sober work. Abner lived with his passion as with a trustworthy enemy. The yearly drinking bout was not preceded by fear, nor was it followed by remorse. He lowered the bars deliberately, without a struggle. He returned to work with a feeling of humility, but also with a sense of confidence.

Sheep never get used to life. They view anything that comes in sight as something outlandish and unprecedented. Though they are undeniably silly, there is something remarkably human about them. Their fear of loneliness is pathetic. One cannot help thinking that, like sheep, human beings herd together in tribes and nations and follow a leader because of their fear of life and their feeling of being eternal strangers in this world.

It was Abner's delight to notice that sheep were not all alike. The leaders were of course conspicuous. What a sight it was to watch a leading sheep, as with outstretched neck it stood, seemingly weighing something in its mind, and then lurched forward, tearing the flock after it. In addition to the leaders, the flock often contained a few outstanding individuals. These were the independent sheep. They were the sheepherder's joy and despair. Abner gave such sheep names, and he would speak of Deborah, Miriam, Judith, Sammy, David, and so on. He spoke of them the way other people tell stories about acquaintances. I remember his story about Miriam, the two-year-old ewe, who was without fear and had a taste for adventure. On his first day with the flock, Abner saw her go off to the creek. When she was through drinking she crossed to the opposite slope and curled up under a scrabby oak. Fuzz, the dog, struck out after her. Abner chuckled when he described what happened next. The barking dog circled around the sheep, but she remained in a posture of unconcern with her head flattened against the ground. The dog became imperious and snapped at her, but he immediately jumped back, yapping shrilly. Abner walked over to investigate. The ewe saw him coming and got up. She recrossed the creek and joined the flock, but without undue haste.

Abner's last job was on the Brewster sheep ranch, south of Tracy. It was there that he came across the wonder sheep Joel, a one-year-old buck with a black muzzle and expressive eyes. From the moment of Abner's arrival Joel began to follow him like a dog. When Fuzz tried to shoo him away, Joel fought back. Eventually Fuzz and Joel became buddies, and Abner entertained the idea of training Joel to leadership. Joel had already learned to lie down and get up at Abner's command. He learned fast. It would be an achievement to have a sheep leader who would follow instructions.

Abner's stay at the Brewster farm was a happy one until he was suddenly overcome by an irresistible craving and got drunk while on the job. Brewster, a decent man, spoke kindly when Abner finally sobered up: "You have to get it out of your system, Abner. You have been keeping to yourself too long. Go to Sacramento or Stockton and stay there a while. See a few movies, and the sight of people in the streets will do you a world of good. A good talk is sometimes all that's needed to chase the devil that drives us to drink. I was a boozer myself, but I cut it all out. It can be done. Come back as soon as you have taken hold of yourself. You know that I value you, both as a worker and as a friend."

Joel and Fuzz stood looking at Abner as if they knew the import of the old man's words. Abner said, "I recommend Joel to your care, Mr. Brewster. He is a fine animal. I leave Fuzzy too; he will be happier here." He led Joel into the enclosed meadow and chained Fuzz to the pepper tree. He then shouldered his bedroll and took the trail to the highway. Joel kept running along the fence, bleating loudly. Abner halted a moment, then jerking his hand in resignation trudged on.

My acquaintance with Abner Ward lasted about three
weeks. We usually got together during his sober intervals. It
did not seem that he would stop drinking, as he had done in
the past when his money gave out, and find a new job. He
kept talking incessantly and I found his talk interesting. I was
a good listener.

One day in late April, as Abner was about to cross the
tracks, a freight train pulled in from the south and blocked
the crossing. It was a mixed train of tank cars, boxcars, and
cattle cars. The train began to move and then stopped abruptly with much rattling and shaking, as the engine broke loose
with a string of tank cars. When the din subsided, Abner's
frazzled nerves were suddenly taut. His feverish eyes saw one
of the cattle cars laden with lambs. A pungent whiff of sheep
was in his nostrils. He judged by the vigorous bleating that
they had not traveled far. He went near the car and peered at
the lambs through the slots. They were restless and terribly
crowded. He surmised that they were on a short trip, probably to a slaughterhouse in Stockton. As his eyes flitted over
the mosaic of wooly backs he noticed, near the far end of the
car, a black monkey-face raised above the wavy mass like the
head of a swimmer. It was baaing with all its might as it
pushed slowly through the thick of the bodies. "Joel!" The
word exploded in Abner's head. There was an infernal crash
as again the engine backed into the train, and Abner had to
jump back. The cars began to roll. Abner let out a piercing
yell, and ran groggily after the car. A brakie on the iron
ladder of a boxcar shouted at him and waved him away. But
Abner ran on, stumbling and shouting. The switch engine
broke loose with a string of boxcars, and the remaining cars,
including the one with the lambs, rolled backward until they
came to a standstill.

A crowd had gathered to watch the shouting, crying

drunk as he fumbled with the levers and air hose in a clumsy attempt to uncouple the sheep car. The brakie, running on top of the cars, jumped on him, and Abner, with one blow, knocked him out. Another brakie fared no better, and the yard policeman was kicked in the stomach, and he too passed out. And all the time Abner was sobbing, "That bastard Brewster promised to take care of Joel, and now they are going to slaughter him." He did not succeed in uncoupling the car but broke open the sliding door of the car. The sheep came jumping, falling on each other. In the meantime, a dozen policemen and members of the crew overpowered Abner, and he was led off to jail. Next day, when I tried to see him, I was told that he was transferred to a nuthouse in Stockton.

22

IT WAS late afternoon when our freight train pulled into Fresno's railroad yard. We were hungry and weary, with no idea of what would be ahead of us. Automatically we drifted toward the State Free Employment Agency, although we knew that it would be closed this time of day. We sat on the steps of the agency, staring listlessly into the twilight. Suddenly a small black Ford pulled up in front of us. The driver, a tall, elderly man, came over. He smiled and said, "I am lucky! I need all the men I can get to help with the haying." We piled into the car, and he drove us into the dark.

I could not see much of Arthur Kunze's farm when we got there. I saw a whitewashed small house with lighted windows and several large shacks. Kunze showed us our bunks, and a woman cook gave us cold cuts and coffee in the dining shack. I remember hearing loud meowing out in the dark. It was the noise made by peacocks nestling in the trees.

I stayed about two months on Kunze's farm. Kunze ate with us and encouraged conversation. Sometimes the conversation grew heated. Kunze hated F.D.R. "He is undermining the character of the country and is turning us into a nation of beggars." The food was excellent and plentiful.

There was a small library in a corner of the dining shack. You had to sign your name in a ledger when you took out a book and when you returned it. I suggested to Kunze that he should get textbooks on all the sciences for those of us who wanted to educate ourselves. He was interested in my ideas about self-education. He asked me about my plans for the future and about the way I was living.

One evening Kunze invited me to the house. He gave me a drink and a cigar. His curiosity about my life as a migratory worker had a strange intensity. Why should a man of my intelligence waste his life? "Before you know it you'll be a helpless, penniless old man. How can you live without a sense of security?" He did not wait for an answer and began to tell me the story of his life. It was a fantastic story.

Kunze was born in Wisconsin. He came to San Francisco in 1882, at the age of seventeen, and went to work in a lumberyard. There, one day, he witnessed a scene which burned itself into his mind and infused him with a passion which shaped his life. The yard foreman, a bull-necked young man, was giving a hand to a gaunt old man in sorting a pile of timbers. The old man was lifting his end of a short piece, when suddenly he let go of it. His fingers had gone stiff. The timber fell with a clatter and barely missed the foreman's toes. The foreman blew his top. "You old son of a bitch! Get the hell out of here. This is not a home for the aged. I ought to kick your ass out of the yard." The old man stood like one in a trance, gazing in wonder at his stiff fingers.

The day of the incident was Kunze's last in the lumberyard. He found a job as a clerk in a hardware store. He now had a goal and was pursuing it with ardor. The vision of the snarling foreman drove him to make money. He was manager of the store at twenty-five and the head of a large hardware corporation at forty. He accumulated a considerable fortune and finally felt secure. No one would dare kick Kunze in the ass.

Then, at the age of fifty-seven, Kunze lost his faith in money, and the sickening fear of a snarling foreman threatening to kick his behind returned in full force. News of the

postwar inflation in Germany and other European countries
threw Kunze into a panic. The green dollar bills, instead of
being an emblem of security, seemed to him now the messen-
gers of impending disaster. He paid a hurried visit to Germany and watched the demoralizing effects of worthless currency. The white thousand-mark banknotes, once the depository
of dreams and of a power that knew no resistance, were now
little better than pieces of paper. You needed now millions of
marks to buy a loaf of bread. In Kunze's eyes this was the
greatest catastrophe the world had seen, greater than the
world war and the Bolshevik revolution. There was a sickening ugliness, and something akin to obscenity, about this van-
ishing of money into thin air. Kunze called on the American
ambassadors in Berlin, Paris, and London. Did they realize
what was happening? The fate of Western civilization and of
Christianity was dangling on a thin thread. The people who
had seen their savings and hard-earned money vanish into
nothingness would lose faith in our civilization and institu-
tions.

Kunze decided that only those who raised their own bread
and meat could have a measure of security. Thus Kunze's
passionate pursuit of security turned him into a farmer.

I laughed when Kunze finished his tale. He looked surprised. "I can't understand you," he said. "Have you never a
thought of the future? How can an intelligent person live
without a sense of security?"

I answered seriously, "You won't believe it, but my future
is far more secure than yours. You think your farm gives you
safety. But come the revolution, you won't have a farm. On
the other hand, as a migratory worker I have nothing to worry about. No matter what happens to the currency and the
social system, sowing and harvesting will go on, and I'll be
needed. If you want absolute security, go on the bum and

learn how to earn a living as a migratory worker." It seemed a wonderful joke, and we both laughed.

About a year later, during the apple-picking season, as I was waiting for a train that would take me to Sebastopol, I noticed among the waiting crowd a tall, elderly man with a bedroll. There was something very familiar about him. He looked like somebody I had known. I tried to remember, and suddenly the word "Kunze" exploded in my head.

I could not restrain myself and called out, "Hello, Mr. Kunze."

He looked at me, surprised. "My name is Siegert," he said.

"Well," I said, "you are the exact duplicate of a million-aire farmer near Fresno. His name is Kunze. You could pass for him anywhere. Think what we could do! We could kidnap Kunze, put you in his place, and no one would know the difference. We could live happily ever after."

We both laughed. He said, "Every man has at least a thousand people in the world who look like him. Have you never come across someone who looked like your identical twin?"

I agreed and told him the story of Bill. I asked him whether he would mind if I went on calling him Kunze. He laughed. "Call me anything you want."

We traveled together for a while, then parted when I took a train to southern California. He was good company. I came across him several times during the following months. Then I completely lost sight of him. During the next ten years or so I had no thought of Kunze, until one day I saw on the front page of *The Fresno Bee* the announcement of his death. The Sunday edition of the *Bee* had the text of Kunze's will, which to me was a fantastic document. This was a new Kunze, wholly different from the man who had a pathological fear of the future. The new Kunze was mature and wise. The most striking items were the two at the end of the will.

One provided five hundred thousand dollars for the fostering of creative work, in music and the arts, in Fresno County: "Prizes of not less than a thousand dollars each should be awarded to persons living in the County of Fresno who compose a worthy piece of music or produce a work of art in any medium. I hope that persons well on in years will try for the prizes. We are on the way of becoming a nation of middle-aged people and I see no harm in it. But we must find ways of stirring and maintaining a creative vigor in older people. We must reject the preposterous assumption that at forty a man is a finished product incapable of new beginnings. There is no evidence that at forty a man learns or unlearns less readily than an adolescent. Certainly, the middle-aged are more sensitive, more conscious of the preciousness of life, and more patient in observation and execution. Our economic system makes it necessary for a man to spend half of his life in securing a steady source of income. There is half a lifetime left for the erection of a super-structure. But not one in a million puts his hand to it. Retirement with us is a travesty and a cruel joke. It is an indictment of the American way of life that our declining years are soured by boredom and disappointment. Old age should be the fruit of a man's life, sweet and fragrant.

"Let, therefore, the middle-aged and the old in Fresno County try their hand with brush and paint. No one has put on canvas the combination of grayish pink and pale gold which colors our hills in early summer. No one has caught the immense variety of greens—the green of vineyards, the individual greens of almond, peach, apricot, plum, orange and olive trees, the greens of wheat, oat, clover and alfalfa fields, of meadows and tule swamps. Our soils, too, are black, gray, red, brown and in patches even bluish gold.

"As to music. There must be thousands of new melodies dormant in the hearts of the inhabitants of our county. Lure the melodies into the light, sing or play them, and if they have a touch of life they should win awards. If you learn the art of musical notation you could record the twitter of birds, the whisper of the wind in the leaves, the humming of bees, the bubbling of water in streams and irrigation ditches, the howling of the west wind, the patter of rain drops, and the sad wailing of a train as it plumbs the depths of the silent night."

The last item in Kunze's will had a dash of humor. It provided $40,000 for the establishment and maintenance of a hobo "jungle" on fifteen acres of land within walking distance of Fresno's railroad yard. The shelter was to have two wings, separated by a court. One wing would be equipped with showers and the other with sinks for washing clothes. In the court there were to be built-in camp stoves. A pile of stove wood was to be kept outside the court. On the lintel of the court gate there was to be a painted mural showing God on his throne, surrounded by angels and faced with Satan in the guise of a hobo shouldering a bedroll. Carved underneath the mural would be a quotation from the Book of Job: "And the Lord said unto Satan: 'Whence comest thou?' And Satan said: 'From going to and fro in the land, and from walking up and down it.'"

23

It is easier to understand a similarity than to explain a difference. A child can understand why man has much in common with other living things. But when trying to explain the uniqueness of man, one is up against the insoluble mystery of the origin of language. So, too, it is easy to understand why France and Germany, two adjoining countries, should have much in common, but it is difficult to explain the striking difference between them. Again, it is easy to understand why the ancient Hebrews had so much in common with the Phoenicians and other neighboring countries but, so far, no one has explained why the Hebrews alone invented a one-and-only God and became a one-and-only people, unlike any other people on earth.

Whenever I come up against something unique, I feel that there is a secret hidden somewhere that must be nosed out. When you travel down the San Joaquin Valley you are struck by the uniqueness of the town of Modesto. You pass through a string of small towns—Turlock, Modesto, Madera, Merced— all having the same climate, raising the same crops, and inhabited by the same type of people. But only Modesto has the most beautiful lawns in Christendom. The town is a vast lawn dotted with houses, and its inhabitants seem to be occupied full time mowing the lawns. You notice that when a lawn invades the cement sidewalk, no one stops it. The park commission has bred an ash tree that sheds all its leaves in one week, so the lawns are kept free of the debris of dying leaves.

How come the lawns of Modesto? I wandered for days through the streets, trying to nose out the secret. I found no clue. I asked the people in the city hall and in the office of the local paper, and got no answer. Nobody knew. I went to the library but did not find a history of Modesto. Then one day, by sheer chance, or perhaps prompted by the unconscious logic that if the living have no answers you interrogate the dead, I went to the cemetery. I found that the oldest graves were of people who came from the County of Essex in southeast England, where lawns were probably invented.

My feeling is that similarities are natural, but differences are made by men. Sometimes we know the names of the men who initiated the difference, but most often these men are buried in unmarked and unvisited graves. History is made not by irresistible forces but by example.

It pleases me no end when I find that common, everyday happenings shed light on history. Perhaps the trouble with our written histories is that the historians derive their insights into the past from the study of ancient relics and documents and not from the study of the present. No historian I know of will accept the fact that the present illumes the past rather than the other way around. Most historians take no interest in what is happening before their eyes.

24

IT IS the mark of a creative artist that he makes the familiar seem new. In my case, fate was the artist.

I remember working for a hard-driving farmer in northern California. He felt cheated any time we paused to catch our breath while haying, though he breathed his horses at frequent intervals. We worked ten hours a day, long after the horses had been returned to their barn.

One evening after a hard day's work I caught sight of my face in a piece of mirror somebody had hung on the wall behind the wash trough. I was startled by my wild and worried appearance. Without stopping to think, I ran to get my bedroll and asked the farmer for my pay. He looked surprised, but managed to scrape together fifty-some dollars, mostly in one-dollar bills. The Sacramento bus was due any moment, so I did not stop to stash away the bills. I reached the highway just as the bus hove into sight. I waved my fistful of bills, and the bus stopped. As I found my seat I kept staring at the bills. I suddenly felt that what I had in my fist were not prosaic dollar bills but a wondrous charm. All I had to do was wave the charm and the world would do my bidding. I had waved it to stop the bus, and later in Sacramento I would wave it and people would come running to bathe, clothe, feed, and bed me. To each who did my bidding, I would give a piece of the charm.

For over two weeks, until the money was gone, life seemed a fairy tale. I suddenly realized how momentous an invention money was. It was an indispensable step in the advancement of humanity; in the emergence of freedom and equality. In a moneyless society there is no freedom of choice, since it is ruled by sheer power, and no equality, since brute force cannot be distributed. Money power can be controlled without coercion.

When you consider the role played by Jews, a weak minority, and by the merchant class while still under the heels of feudal lords in the development of banking, it will seem plausible that money was invented by the weak. The wielders of absolute power have always hated money. They expect people to be motivated by noble ideals and end up by using terror to keep things going. The moment money ceases to play a dominant role, there will be an end to automatic progress. The breakdown of civilization will be marked by a breakdown of currencies. Money and profit-making may seem trivial and mean. But everyday life is likely to be meager and difficult where people will act and strive only when animated by noble motives.

Familiarity dulls the cutting edge of life. It is perhaps a mark of the artist that he is an eternal stranger in this world, a visitor from another planet.

25

Pearl harbor put an end to my life as a migratory worker. I rushed to San Francisco to help win the war. By sheer luck the State Free Employment Agency dispatched me to the Longshoreman's Union. Chance has shaped my life and never more so than in my becoming a longshoreman. There are many things longshoremen and migratory workers have in common. Neither on the road nor on the docks is there such a thing as a steady job. There is a good chance that if you work seven days a week on the docks you'll be working on seven different ships for seven different bosses and with different people. The members of the union presented the same ethnic mixture I had met on the road. Thus the shift from the road to the docks was not a drastic change. I felt at home in the union from the first day.

I also found the union mentally stimulating. As I watched it in action I kept thinking about the uniqueness of America and about the mechanics of the historic process. The union is run by nobodies. Every longshoreman could become a president of the union. It was exciting to watch a barely literate longshoreman acting as president and doing his job competently. There were a few intellectuals in the union, and invariably they felt frustrated and angry when a common longshoreman was elected to high office and performed tolerably well. It did not occur to them that it was part of America's uniqueness that in this country nobodies perform tasks which in other countries are reserved for elites. Like America, the union was founded by a leader. Harry Bridges is a sort of Jefferson. And like Jefferson, he created an organization that functions well without leaders.

At first sight it seemed paradoxical that an organization operated by common people should be so exclusive. It was only during the war that the union opened its doors to new-comers. In normal times, entrance into the Longshoreman's Union is more difficult than entrance into an exclusive aristo-cratic club. Actually, it is a sentimental notion that common people are more ready to share than are educated people. What a common man craves most is to become an aristocrat.

I also speculated on the role common people played in history. Up to the end of the eighteenth century, common people were passive clay in the hand of elites. The birth of America and the coming of the French Revolution marked the entrance of nobodies onto the stage of history. The revo-lutions of the twentieth century are a reaction against history made by common people. It was easier for a common man to achieve high office in czarist than in Lenin's Russia. All through the nineteenth century the intellectuals made war against democratic societies, and they won the war in the twentieth. The victorious intellectuals often establish more absolutist regimes than did their predecessors. The life of common people in societies dominated by intellectuals is not unlike the life they lived in the Middle Ages, the golden age of elites.

My twenty-five years as a longshoreman were a fruitful interval in my life. I learned to write and published several books. My becoming a writer did not impress anybody in the union. Every longshoreman believes that there is nothing he could not do if he took the trouble.

26

DID I EVER have moments of complete happiness? My life with Helen was certainly happy, and I savored a rare moment of incomparable happiness when she came out of the darkness of past midnight into the cafeteria, threw her arms around me, and kissed me. Nevertheless, the happiness of that rare moment was not unalloyed. It was shot through with a nagging sense of inadequacy and doubts about my worthiness.

No! The only moment of unalloyed happiness I ever had was when I received a wire from Harper telling me that they would publish *The True Believer*. I felt like a darling of fate, an immortal raised above the common run of humanity. There were no doubts about my worthiness and no fear about the future.

Fortunately, I had no one to share my elation with. This might have turned a momentary feeling of superiority into a durable conviction. As it was, I soon cooled off and eventually shared the prevailing opinion on the waterfront that any longshoreman could write a great book if he took the trouble. I cannot remember when and in what order my other books appeared. I write because I must. I do not think of myself as a writer.

It is the testimony of the ages that there is little happiness—least of all when we get what we want. Many outstanding persons who reviewed their lives in old age found that all their happy moments did not add up to a full day.

Did I have moments of total unhappiness? Not moments, but years of unrelieved unhappiness after I ran away from Helen: The break affected both mind and body. As I said before, I have never fully recovered.

27

I HAVE never had a grievance. It has always seemed to me that the world has treated me better than I have deserved. This was strikingly demonstrated during my sole experience of physical attack. A drunken Mexican cut my right thigh from the crotch to the knee. It burned him up that I was the only sober person in a barrack where everybody was roaring drunk. I remember that my first thought was not to kill the Mexican but how to get immediately to a hospital. During my stay in the hospital I gave no thought to the Mexican. I was told he was in prison.

Months later, as I clambered to the top of a moving box-car, I saw someone jump to the next car while looking at me over his shoulder. He kept on running and jumping. It was the Mexican. I felt like reassuring him that he had nothing to be afraid of. In this country it is considered manly to retaliate and avenge oneself. I don't know how I would have behaved if the physical attacks were frequent. But I was usually left alone, due probably to my size.

I remember witnessing a dramatic instance of retaliation. I was given a ride on a truck going to Placerville. As I settled beside the driver I heard a loud hissing. Was the carburetor overheated? Then I saw that the hissing came from a cage full of rattlesnakes. The cage, made of tight mesh wire, was at the feet of the driver. Strange cargo. The driver did not say a word. When we reached Placerville the truck stopped in front of a saloon, and the driver carried the cage inside. A minute later I heard a loud commotion and saw people tumbling out of the saloon, laughing and cussing. I soon learned what had happened. Weeks before, the truck driver had got drunk and was thrown out onto the pavement by the saloon keeper. He now retaliated by letting loose a cageful of rattlesnakes, and he was wrecking the joint in the confusion.

It could be that my readiness to forgive others is a device for making it possible to forgive myself. For hand in hand with my unwillingness to nurse a grievance goes a total incapacity for feeling remorse.